With the Compliments of the Author.

ONE MOLE RAMPANT.

BY

W. G.

The Naval & Military Press Ltd

Published by

The Naval & Military Press Ltd

Unit 5 Riverside, Brambleside
Bellbrook Industrial Estate
Uckfield, East Sussex
TN22 1QQ England

Tel: +44 (0)1825 749494

www.naval-military-press.com
www.nmarchive.com

To H.G., whose character, judgment and courage have ever been a source of inspiration.

PREFACE

As the Preface is usually skipped by readers, this only contains what might well be so treated :

What a queer title !

Well, all soldiers were moles, more or less, in this war, burrowing in the ground. Some more than others.

But why " Rampant " ?

Well, wouldn't it make you ramp too?

CONTENTS

MAPS

INTRODUCTION

THIS represents an attempt to reconstruct a more or less coherent account of one man's experiences on Active Service. The Mole's period of service at the front was just short of a year, when he was recalled to England to take up other duties in connection with the war. His experiences are, therefore, limited in comparison with those of many others, but as they include quite an early part of the war and some features of it familiar only to comparatively few, it may nevertheless form a record of some interest.

For a description of training in England read Ian Hay's classic, "The First Hundred Thousand," and for general atmosphere at the front readers cannot do better than turn to "Between the Lines" and "Action Front," by Boyd Cable, "Men, Women and Guns" and "No Man's Land," by Sapper, and for realism to "Under Fire," the translation from the French "Le Feu," by M. Henri Barbusse.

In letters home the darker side of war was always minimised, partly on account of the Censor and partly because one did not want to add to the

inevitable worry of the people at home. But let
there be no mistake about it. War is a horrible
thing, and the suffering is terrible, not only directly
as the result of wounds, but even worse, because
much more inevitable and continuous, from the
discomforts, amounting at times to agony. Many
a man has longed for a " Blighty " wound that
would disable him sufficiently to take him out of
the drear round of cold, wet and exposure. Fortunately the human mind and body is elastic, and
even in billets, where the comfort consists chiefly
of a roof over one's head within sound of gunfire,
men can absorb themselves in some trifling recrea-
tion, as a game of cards, a newly-arrived news-
paper, an impromptu sing-song, and forget (literally) that " there is a war on."

Speaking at the City Temple some time ago,
John Oxenham—who described the " Cities of
Death " that he had seen in Flanders and Northern
France—said that the reticence of our soldiers in
regard to the horrors they experienced was the
most loving conspiracy of silence the world had
ever known.

This is only partially correct; it is true that
few men are willing (or able) to describe in
unvarnished language the most offensive sights or
incidents witnessed. For one thing, the soldier
knows that no mere words will ever convey anything like a correct impression of his experiences
to one who has never undergone anything similar;

and, besides that, most men cannot bring themselves to attempt it, from some queer sort of English feeling that "it isn't done." French writers are not hampered in this way.

On top of this, the characteristic defect of the average Tommy, who is, in fact, the average Briton, is in some directions a lack of imagination —a trait which at the same time is his great virtue, enabling him to ignore anything but the immediate present.

Finally, the vocabulary of our "Tommy" is strictly limited, and in most cases he will merely describe his experiences as "b——y awful."

CHAPTER I

JOINING UP

ALTHOUGH the actual outbreak of hostilities seems to have come as a " bolt from the blue " to many people, who in numerous cases had just started for the Continent on their holidays, others saw with gloomy disquiet, particularly during the week preceding the August Bank Holiday (August 3rd, 1914), what seemed to be inevitably coming. That was a week of sinister apprehension which brooded over all one's thoughts and actions. The fateful threat of war was like a gradually approaching thunder-cloud which nothing could stave off. To the Mole, at least, it was almost a relief from a tension which was growing intolerable when England finally declared war, though he did not share the common misapprehension that it was going to be a matter of months and an easy victory for the Allies. But no man at that time had any conception of what efforts would be called for.

Kitchener's appeal to join " for three years or for the duration of the war " was met by a flood of men with which the recruiting offices were unable to cope. Men waited for hours in queues, sometimes day after day, trying to enlist. The age limit was fixed at 30. Under the circumstances the Mole, who had no wish to serve unless it was absolutely necessary, and who was already over the age limit, sought other outlets for useful activities. He was able to be of some assistance driving a private car for the military authorities, and was attached for a week or so in that capacity to the newly-formed Naval Division at Deal. Amongst other people he piloted round was Lambert, the Civil Lord of the Admiralty. The Naval Division was the child of Winston Churchill's brain, the idea apparently being to utilise superfluous naval forces, such as the Naval Volunteers and the Fleet Reserve, as a military body, a decision which roused much dissent and also caused considerable resentment amongst the officers and men involved. Two brigades were formed, under Henderson and Backhouse respectively, who held the rank of Commodore, equivalent to Brigadier-general. Besides the Mole, a Mr. M. had also come with his car to act in a like capacity. " Winston " himself ran down from London one day in his Rolls-Royce. Mr. M. and the Mole were introduced by the Brigade Commanders, who were good enough to express their appreciation of the useful services performed.

After the Mole had joined up, as he heard in 1917, M. received a commission as Captain and continued acting as driver. He went with the Naval Division on the ill-starred Antwerp expedition, only narrowly escaping internment in Holland, as actually happened to Henderson and a large body of men under his command. M. also accompanied the Naval Division to Egypt, and eventually to Gallipoli, finally relinquishing his commission on account of ill-health.

In the meantime the Press kept reporting successful engagements of the enemy by the Belgians and French. So August drew to a close. Then towards the end of the month came the famous issue of *The Times* with the first intimation of the Retreat from Mons (Battle of Mons started August 23rd). Things looked very black. The age limit was raised to 35, and the Mole decided that the time had come when the country required every able-bodied man for the fighting units. There seemed to be little prospect of obtaining a commission without O.T.C. experience; only about 2,000 were then being granted, and the Military Authorities had issued a statement that those joining up in the ranks would not prejudice their chance of obtaining a commission by doing so; on the contrary, they would receive special consideration. This, by the way, like many other official announcements, proved to be false. The Mole, therefore, made up his mind to join as a "Tommy." He had no illusions as to military glory and knew from previous experiences roughing it what hardships might be expected. His only motive was the feeling that every able-bodied man left in London should be asked to produce his reasons in writing.

Now came the choice of regiment. The Mole said that he did not mind taking his chance of being potted, but did not like the idea of bunking in with the "Great Unwashed." He, therefore, endeavoured to get into the H.A.C.

On Monday, August 31st, he called on Mr. D., a late member of the H.A.C., and obtained a letter of introduction to the Council and presented it at Armoury House, Finsbury. Here also it was no easy matter to be accepted for enlistment, and some men were several days about it. A man had to be introduced by a member of the H.A.C., or vouched for by two householders, and a subscription of two guineas was required. In reply to questions the Mole stated that he was willing to volunteer for service abroad (enlistment in a Territorial unit being otherwise for home service) and was willing to be a pioneer, the only vacancy left in the 1st Battalion; this without having the foggiest notion of what the duties of a pioneer were—a good many others were equally unenlightened—but it sounded something akin to engineering, with which he was familiar. He was then medically examined in a perfunctory sort of way, the doctor mostly taking his word for it that he was fit. Then a lunch in a nearby restaurant; and, later, accepted, he paid the subscription and was attested. The swearing-in was done by a short-sighted "dug-out," who, in his attempt to read off the oath to the new recruit, actually read the portion certifying that he, a magistrate or other duly authorised officer, had attested Blank this Blank day, all of which the Mole solemnly repeated, realising what was happening but letting it go at that. The error was only discovered when the signature was to be appended, but as the Mole then said he considered himself as having taken the oath of allegiance, the officer was satisfied. Finally he signed the " Buff Form," the cause of much objurgation amongst the men in later days, by which he volunteered for service abroad, no matter where. It was the object of much speculation as to where the battalion would be ordered to. General opinion was that they would have at least several months' training in England and then go to relieve garrison troops in Malta or Egypt.

The Mole was now a fully fledged member of the Honourable Artillery Company—Private No. 1711, No. 4 Company, 1st Infantry Battalion. He reported to his Company Commander, Captain C., about five that afternoon, learned that he should provide himself with certain articles, such as knife, fork, spoon, etc., and obtained a day's leave to attend to these and other matters.

Tuesday, September 1st, was a day of scurry and bustle, hasty shopping, arranging kit, winding up affairs, etc., and on Wednesday morning began the tremendous uncertainty as to future movements which always reigns in the Army. The Mole left home to report at Finsbury, not knowing when he would return there. On arrival at Armoury House he was placed under Pioneer Sergt. P. with nine others, forming the pioneer section. No one from the C.O. and Adjutant down had any definite idea for months what pioneers were supposed to do except to use them as generally handy men. Apparently the section, with the exception of the sergeant, had never existed in peace times in the H.A.C. While at Finsbury their chief activities were on the lines of housemaids' work, keeping the parade ground and rooms clean, etc., in which they were assisted by much disgusted professional bandsmen, who protested their job was to *play* not to *work*, and sundry other men on fatigue duty.

The Mole himself, though without any military experience, took charge of a small party of these men once or twice.

It appears that in the ordinary course of events pioneers are trained soldiers who are selected as having some skill as artisans. They are not required to drill and are exempt from fatigues. This tradition persisted, but, as the section soon found that the work of the pioneers might all be regarded as fatigues, there did not seem to be much in it.

Sergt. P. was an amiable, middle-aged gentleman, an architect by profession and a member of the H.A.C. for years. His hobby was musketry, and he was a first-class shot. As an N.C.O., though well-meaning and hard-working, he had a difficult task. His lot was not made any easier by the fact that he was always being worried by Captain D., the Adjutant. D. turned out to be quite a good soldier when at the Front after relinquishing his duties as Adjutant, but while occupying that position he was, although regarded with considerable awe, nevertheless the object of a good deal of derision, his personal peculiarities—a lanky figure and thin, reedy voice—lending themselves to burlesque. One of the songs of the day was from a popular Palace Revue and ran : " I'm Gilbert the Filbert, the Colonel of the Nuts " (sung by the late Basil Hallam, R.F.C.). This was parodied to " I'm Duggy the Adjy, the Beau of Finsburree." The O.C. Battalion was Lieut.-Colonel T., commonly known as Taffy.

The H.A.C. comprises infantry and artillery. Of the latter the Mole saw nothing as the batteries had already been sent elsewhere for training. Subsequently they went to Egypt. The infantry battalion at the outbreak of war had a strength of probably 400 to 500. Recruiting soon brought this up to full strength, about 1,000, all of whom had volunteered for foreign service, while those who did not so volunteer, and surplus new recruits, formed a 2nd Battalion. The original members were fairly well trained men, having gone through the usual Territorial drills and camps. They were immediately mobilised and mostly used for guard duties, sentries on the railway, detachments at Bermondsey, etc. (always referred to with the accent on the middle). They carried out these guards for several

weeks, and in some cases it got on the men's nerves
to such an extent that they would get up out of
their sleep and turn out for duty though they were
not called at all. A number of the original members were also made N.C.O.'s and granted commissions in the H.A.C. to deal with the greatly
enlarged numbers, it being a tradition of the
Regiment that all officers are selected from its
own ranks.

By the time the Mole enlisted most of the new
recruits had received a fair amount of instruction
in rudimentary drill, though both officers and men
were far from being highly trained. On one occasion a company on a route march got mixed up
with the Changing of the Guard at the Palace and
got into the most awful confusion.

Both the pioneers and the rest of the men were
occupied for only a few hours in the morning and
afternoon, and there was a lot of hanging about
with nothing much to do. Men amused themselves as best they could, at the canteen, playing
the piano and singing, etc. The pioneers had
intervals when they could watch the others drilling, and so the Mole picked up a few ideas of the
various commands. Nearly all were dismissed
about five, and the Mole found that he could
return home.

On Thursday morning the Mole again left the
house, not knowing what developments the day
would bring forth. The first event of the morning

was roll-call on the parade ground. This was conducted with a good deal of ceremony, the H.A.C.
always modelling themselves on the Guards, with
whom they were accustomed to be brigaded in
previous wars. The men fell in and dressed their
lines with much, apparently, quite unnecessary
jostling up and down, now to the left, now to the
right, and repeat for a period of several minutes to
a roll of drums, finally becoming petrified at the
sharp word of command. This was the subject of
a very amusing burlesque later on in billets. After
parade they broke up into squads for drill and instruction, the pioneers carrying out much the same
duties as before.

The parade ground at Finsbury is quite large.
At one end were the horse-lines, used and attended
to by the regimental transport, then came some
twenty tents, finally the large open space remaining between these and Armoury House. The tents
were used by a comparatively small number of
men sleeping there at night. The transport consisted of a motley collection of vehicles hastily
withdrawn from civil uses, including a sort of dog-
cart boldly labelled "Gorringe, Buckingham
Palace Road," all of which they retained for some
time after reaching France on active service, the
Gorringe cart being used as officers' mess-cart.
Most of these were eventually replaced by G.S.
(General Service) limbers before leaving the advanced base, but "Gorringe" persisted long after

that even, and it was not until well into 1915 that
the battalion was supplied with travelling cookers.
Up to that time all cooking was done in " Dixies,"
oblong iron pots used for cooking stew, making
tea, etc., and usually resulting in each particular
brew tasting somewhat of the previous effort, such
as tea à l'onion. This, however, is anticipating
events.

It was on this day, Thursday, that the Mole
got into uniform, hitherto being in his own
" civvies." There was a great scarcity of uniforms,
and only foreign service men could hope to get one
at all. Even afterwards in the field there was considerable difficulty in getting supplies, partly
caused by the fact that the requirements of the
H.A.C. ran to appreciably larger sizes in tunics
than those of the average soldier. At this time the
home service men, in order to avoid waiting for
weeks, mostly bought their own uniforms privately.
The Mole went to interview the quartermaster-
sergeant, and was duly " issued with " (Army
language) a tunic, trousers, cap and shoulder-
badges, but no cap-badge or puttees were to be
had. He also received a flimsy canvas kit-bag, but
not liking it much, bought from the Q.M.S. one
of a more substantial waterproofed variety, which
was, as a matter of fact, afterwards issued to all
men proceeding overseas. He changed into
uniform and stowed his effects, which he had
brought with him in a suit-case the previous day,

into the kit-bag, packing the mufti into the suit-case.

At noon there was another general parade for dinner. No one was ever quite certain where the pioneers should take up their position. Eventually it was decided that they should fall in with N.C.O.'s behind the drawn up ranks as "super-numeraries." The men would be then numbered off for their different tables in the mess-room. The dinner was excellent food though roughly served. In the middle of the meal came a command, "T'shun, Orderly Officer," and the officer entering would ask if there were any complaints. The day closed as before.

On Friday there was nothing new till the afternoon, when the pioneers were suddenly ordered to hold themselves in readiness to leave early the next morning. They were to proceed to Purfleet, Essex, and were ordered to sleep in the tents that night, being granted leave out until 10 P.M. The Mole dashed off to buy some puttees, and dispatched his suit-case home. He was puzzled after boarding a bus that the conductor seemed to studiously ignore the tendered fare, but suddenly remembered that men in uniform could ride gratis. He was also several times amused and somewhat embarrassed at the cordial way fellow passengers would turn to him as an undoubted authority on all military matters and the prospects of the war.

When turning in that night the Mole undressed,

but although blankets were provided and the weather was warm and dry, it felt pretty chilly, and the ground was hard, so it took some time to get to sleep. He had just dropped off when, as it seemed, in the middle of the night, really about 11, he was told to report up at the house *at once*. Pulling on tunic and trousers over pyjamas, and slipping into unlaced boots, he and the others of the section scrambled there as quickly as possible to find that the adjutant was waiting to see them fitted with greatcoats. These were the grey coats similar to those of the Guards, and at that time with a detachable little cape. It was some time before Duggy's critical eye was satisfied with the length and fit of the coats, and several had to be tried on each man before he would pass him. Then, taking the number of the coat allotted to him, each man drew equipment, rifle and bayonet, all bearing the same number. About 1 A.M. the section were allowed to return to their broken rest. It may here be noted that the greatcoat and cape were carried in a sort of sling, not the present pack, and had to be most cunningly folded in just one particular way to make a satisfactory square appearance. As not one of the pioneers had ever seen it done, let alone be expert at it, they were eventually allowed to withdraw, leaving a sputtering Q.M.S. surveying with wrathful eye a litter of coats and equipment scattered about the floor.

" And so to bed."

CHAPTER II

IN CAMP

ON Saturday, September 5th, the pioneers were
routed out bright and early, dressed and packed
their kit-bags. These were about 2 ft. 6 in. long
and rather over a foot in diameter, tied with a cord
at the top. By bulging them out a surprisingly
large amount of stuff can be squeezed into this
small space, but the Mole found it none too large
for his belongings, and by the time it was full it
was pretty hefty. These bags were turned over
to two transport men who were to be attached
temporarily to the section, and drove a wagon down
with the bags, two tents, blankets, a couple of
dixies, etc. Then to a hurried breakfast, which
was very good. Directly after hasty instruction
was given in packing the greatcoats, and the
pioneers clumsily struggled into their equipment
for the first time. They fell in under the baleful
eye of the adjutant. Now it is one of the jealously
prized privileges of the H.A.C. to march through
the City with bayonets fixed, and no opportunity
of exercising is allowed to pass without the regiment or party availing themselves of it. So the
section "fixed bayonets" with a deplorable lack
of smartness, not surprising as none of them had
ever done it before in their lives, and, finally, fairly
shooed away by Duggy in disgust, got out through

the gate in the best military formation they could muster, and set off to march to Fenchurch Street Station. The time was short (they had to catch an early train), the pace was quick, the sun was hot, and as none were accustomed to the weight of the pack they arrived sweating profusely just in time to unfix bayonets and tumble into the train. Sergt. P., who had been shivering under the unspoken criticisms of Duggy, heaved a profound sigh of relief.

The party later detrained and marched to Belhous Park, which seemed to be part of a private estate. The transport wagon arrived later. The tents were then erected, and the section made their first attempt at cooking. The result, as might be expected, was not altogether a brilliant success. For a long time the Army went on the principle that if you told a man he was cook, he *was* one. It did not always work out, but by experience and trial (*sic*) one managed to get enough to eat, even if not of the most palatable dishes. As one result of the lack of culinary skill, the meals mostly took the form of stew, which even a novice could manage. On a later occasion the Mole acted as cook for forty men for a day. They survived it.

The pioneers were to prepare the camp for the arrival of the remainder later on. They soon found out what every soldier learned early in his service, that the soldier's best friend is his spade, not his rifle. They were very busy and really did credit-

able work. Rations were drawn daily from a near-
by depot in the wagon. The weather was clear and
hot, and they had quite a good time, though all
acquired large and painful blisters. They also got a
little instruction from Sergt. P. in the use and care
of the rifle and some very elementary drill.

[LETTER]

"IN CAMP, *September* 6, 1914.

"We got off all right yesterday morning, arriving here about 10. As it was our first experience
of marching with kit and rifle we were pretty warm.
However, the march was only from the station, so
it was not bad. Our nearest village is Aveley,
P.O. address as follows :—

"Belhous Park, Purfleet."

"We have been very busy preparing camp for
the rest of the battalion, who are to come down
some time next week. There are ten of us here at
present, and we have two tents between us. Little
prospect of leave for some time to come, as there
is so much to do. Food very rough-and-ready, but
not bad. I am sleeping fairly well on the whole.
The weather has been very kind to us so far.

"The men in the pioneer section are all a very
decent lot, and we shall be together most of the
time. I believe as pioneers we get most of the
hard advance work, but have certain other privileges to make up for it. We shall probably be
here some time (two to three months)."

Not far away was a camp of new Kitchener's men. The section heard tales of great dissatisfaction, inadequate accommodation, lack of food, incipient mutiny and desertions, but it was probably much exaggerated, though there is no doubt the authorities were hard put to it to accommodate the ever-growing flood of new recruits. One day the Mole and another pioneer were going with the transport to pick up supplies, when they found two of the "Kitcheners" overcome with heat, surrounded by some of their mates; the party apparently being on field manœuvres. The two unconscious men were loaded on to the wagon and taken to the hospital tent of their camp.

The work at the park progressed, but was fairly uneventful except for one small incident.

Sunday, September 13.—During the night the two horses were tethered to trees. One of them broke loose and kicked out a tent-peg, just behind the Mole's head, making considerable noise generally. A few inches would have made a big difference. With much cursing the occupants of the tent settled down to sleep again.

By this time the Mole had discovered that two things were desirable as conducive to comfort at night—a knitted woollen cap and an air cushion. He also knew from previous experience that when sleeping on the ground a useful tip is to scoop out a hollow for the hip-bone.

All this time the weather was hot and dry.

Water had been laid on and it was possible to wash and even get an improvised shower-bath.

Just about this time another detachment came down to erect tents for the arrival of the battalion. In the meantime preparations were fairly well completed, though there was still a certain amount to do.

Monday, September 14.—The battalion came down.

Before leaving headquarters the H.A.C. was inspected by the King. The Mole heard afterwards that the effect was marred as Taffy, in his excitement, gave the order to " present arms " while the men were at " order arms," i.e., the rifle-butt resting on the ground, instead of first giving the command, " slope hipe," bringing the rifle to the shoulder. This resulted in a distinctly ragged display.

Up to now the weather had been bright and hot, but the day the main body came down it started raining, and the afternoon brought a downpour. Life under canvas may be quite a pleasant picnic when it is fine, but in wet weather it becomes very miserable. Whenever the canvas is touched by any mischance it starts leaking. The ground becomes sodden and churned into mud which is unavoidably tramped into the tents. In a permanent camp tent-boards, forming a wooden floor, may be provided, but at Aveley there was nothing but the ground. In fact there was a considerable shortage

all round. Only one blanket per man was to be
had, and as for "wetter-sheets," a waterproof
ground sheet, two had to suffice for three men.
The number of tents was also limited, and twelve
men had to crowd into one tent. This meant packing in tightly, and the process of preparing for sleep
was extremely complicated. However, miserable
as they were with the wet and the general discomfort, the gymnastics and confusion of turning in
roused the pioneers to shrieks of laughter at the
general congestion that night.

The Army is always a hotbed of rumours,
plausible rumours, impossible ones, sometimes surprisingly accurate and at other times wholly wrong,
but always rumours innumerable. The H.A.C.
soon made up their minds they would eventually
get to the Front in France, but it seemed pretty
definite from the permanent camp that was
arranged that they were good for a stay of at least
some months at Aveley, unless it was terminated
by moving into barracks in the winter months,
Wellington Barracks for choice. With more experience of what Ian Hay calls the " Practical Joke
Department " of the service, they would have had
less confidence in their conclusions. The commissariat arrangements were far from perfect, and the
men went short at times. In a day or so things
began to settle down. Preparations were made
for constructing a miniature rifle range, and everything pointed to a prolonged stay.

CHAPTER III

OFF TO ?

THE battalion had only arrived on Monday when on Wednesday a brand new rumour flashed through the camp : The H.A.C. was ordered to France. Was it true? What about leave? When would they be off? As a matter of fact no leave was granted. Up to this time half the battalion was using the modern webbing equipment, while the other half had the so-called Slade Wallet type with white crossed slings of the old-fashioned kind. On Thursday a supply of the webbing equipment was received and distributed. It was all in its component parts, and to the uninitiated took a lot of fitting together.

Friday, September 18.—Left Aveley 3 A.M. left Southampton 4.30 P.M.

In a letter written later the Mole said :—

" In the hurry and scurry of leaving England there was only just time to advise you of the fact, and it will no doubt interest you to hear about it more fully now.

" About three days before the actual event word went round that we were to leave shortly for some overseas destination. As camp life breeds rumours as rapidly as germs multiply I did not feel certain that it was correct. Even so, we were in doubt as to destination—France, India, Malta?   Later on it was officially announced that we *were* off and also that about two hundred men were to be left behind. There was tremendous excitement as to who would be left.   After the names had been given out new equipment arrived, and all the afternoon and the best part of the evening was spent in drawing it and getting it fitted together.   Then we were told to stand by to exchange our rifles for newer models. As a matter of fact the rifles did not begin turning up until about midnight, and then there was a tremendous helter-skelter getting them unpacked and distributed.   Of course there was no sleep that night.   All this lasted until just about 3 A.M., when the order came to parade for departure.   More flurry !   Kit-bags were packed and turned over to the transport to disappear for several days, and we had only what we could carry on our backs.   We assembled in the dark, and finally marched off to Purfleet Station.   There we were served out with our complement of ammunition, one hundred rounds apiece, and a very small ration of bread and cheese, which had to serve until night, as we afterwards found.   We finally started at 6 A.M.   I went to sleep before we reached London, but I hear we went round by the North and then on to Southampton without any stop.   On arrival there, about 1 P.M., we loaded ship and sailed about 4.30.

"We carried our own transport—horses and

wagons—with us on the ship, also supplies and stuff consigned to other troops. We were convoyed across by various war vessels—English destroyers, armed merchantmen, French cruisers, etc. We heard the captain sailed under sealed orders. The worst of the trip was caused by the fact that the transport horses were stabled immediately above the hold in which we slept, so that the incessant kicking and stamping was very disturbing, to say nothing of the smell.''

CHAPTER IV

FRANCE

[LETTER]

September 20, 1914.

" Arrived off St. Nazaire (?) somewhere in the Bay of Biscay. A little rough, but not as bad as it might have been. A bit sick yesterday morning but all right since. The boat is a refrigerator ship and converted for transport purposes by a few tables in the holds. Sleep anywhere, on or under tables, or any available space. Feeding on hard biscuits and corned beef for past three days, and not much at that. Quite a number of men without full equipment. I fear organisation is none too good. They rushed us off in a tremendous hurry. It seems very strange.

"We are bound for Nantes, but don't know what will happen there. Apparently we are to drop practically everything we possess except overcoats and a few small things in a haversack. In view of this please include a pair of thick socks with the weekly tobacco packet. We must trust to luck that it will reach me. I am handing this to a sailor to be posted on his return to England."

It must be remembered that at this time Calais and Boulogne were abandoned and left practically open to the enemy as it was thought impossible to

defend them.   Even Havre was endangered, and
it was therefore necessary to make St. Nazaire (not
far from Bordeaux) the new base.

Monday, September 21.—In rest camp.

[LETTER]

Camp, September 22, 1914.

On Active Service.

" Just a few lines while opportunity offers.   I
do not expect to have a great deal of time for it.
We are still at the point of disembarkation.   We
were off the harbour about 8 A.M., but did not land
until about 8 P.M.—waiting for the tide, I suppose.
Three of our companies went on up to camp (there
is a big one here, all English).   My own company
was put to work at unloading ships.   It was past
midnight when we finished.   We got a couple of
hours' sleep on the ship and then had to clear out as
she was returning empty, I believe.   Incidentally
we were complimented the following day on parade
for our good work.

" We were the first Volunteer Corps to land in
France.   I suppose we shall be going on protective
service on the docks, railways, etc.   Discipline for
the English troops here is very strict, and any
breaches, such as absence without leave, breaking
out of camp, etc., are punishable with very severe
measures.   As a matter of fact practically no leave
is granted, so we do not see much of the place, nor,
for that matter, have we the time for it.

"We are to shed our kit-bags and only take absolute necessities that we can carry on our backs. I am getting along quite well, though, of course, things are very rough-and-ready. The weather is quite nice, though cold at night. We see a little news through the medium of a small local paper. There seems to be doubt of letters or parcels getting through, but please try."

The H.A.C. afterwards learned to their disgust that the London Scottish had arrived just before them. There was a good deal of rivalry between the two regiments.

[FROM A LATER LETTER]

"Of the trip itself I think I have written fairly fully. On our arrival we were welcomed by a cheering crowd. As you know, we landed in the evening and spent a short time on board again that night, being routed out hastily in the early morning when she was about to sail. There were several large camps at the point of disembarkation, but, being very crowded, my own company took refuge in a casino. The officers located themselves in the ordinary casino part, while we took charge of the little theatre to the rear of it. The seats had been removed and we distributed ourselves around it. The following nights were rather humorous. With some others, I occupied the stage, some slept in the

orchestra, and the majority were scattered over the
' audience.' ''

From this casino No. 4 Company went to the
nearby main camp to draw rations at meal-times.
The supply of water was small, being brought in
tank-carts and chiefly limited to drinking purposes.
For washing and bathing troops were taken a few
miles away for a dip in the sea from time to time,
and the H.A.C. had one bathe like this.

Tuesday, September 22.—Up all night awaiting
orders. No. 3 Company left and, as we heard
afterwards, went on to Nantes.

Wednesday, September 23.—Left. No. 4
Company stays.

The pioneers who had been temporary attached
to their respective companies were again re-
assembled as a section. Kit-bags, parted with since
leaving Aveley, reappeared for a few hours only,
to be given up again when under orders to move.
By this time the Mole had learned enough to keep
what he considered essential about him. Having
tried to shave with a borrowed ordinary razor and
without a mirror on board ship, his shaving tackle
being in his kit-bag, and achieving a very inadequate effect, he made up his mind not to get caught
like that again. So when the order to pack up
and stand by for moving came he was this time
better prepared.

It may here be incidentally mentioned that the

new rifles issued to the H.A.C. were packed with grease, and when ordered to parade everyone was in a quandary as to whether the barrel should be cleaned out or left like that for better protection against sea air. The Mole appealed to an N.C.O. for guidance, but that worthy merely replied, " I don't know, and anyway *my* rifle won't be inspected." Most men left the grease untouched, and it was not criticised.

After a night of standing by, it was so cold without any blankets under canvas that men turned out at dawn to move about to restore circulation.

The party finally entrained Wednesday morning for an unknown destination. One of the men asked the Colonel how long the journey would be and, as might be expected, received only a non-committal answer. " Well," said he, " can I take my boots off ? "

" I expect so," said Taffy, " I am going to ! "

CHAPTER V

THE ADVANCE BASE

DISPATCH of Lord French, dated September 17th, 1914.

Speaking of the position on August 29th, he says :—

" The right flank of the German Army was now reaching a point which appeared seriously to endanger my line of communications with Havre. I had already evacuated Amiens, into which place a German Reserve Division was reported to have moved.

" Orders were given to change the base to St. Nazaire, and establish an advance base at Le Mans."

Thursday, September 24.—Arrived Le Mans about 1 A.M., and marched to a camp under canvas.

In a letter of that date the Mole wrote :—

" I cannot tell you about our movements, except to say that we have had an experience of a troop-train journey. After waiting up all night expecting to leave our last camp, we finally entrained about noon the other day. We travelled in a cattle-truck (' 8 chevaux 40 hommes '), made

more or less habitable by some boards serving as
benches. As you can imagine, the springing was
none too good. We arrived at our destination in
the middle of the night (very little sleep again),
and are in temporary camp.

" For the present we have regained our kit-
bags, I am glad to say. The packs are pretty
heavy, and marching any distance is quite an under-
taking. My work as pioneer keeps me pretty busy
attending to necessary jobs around camp.

" Our equipment consists of rifle, bayonet, a
small trenching-tool, water-bottle, haversack for
carrying immediate necessities, such as shaving kit,
soap, etc., mess-tin in three parts, which serve as
plates and mug, etc., and the pack itself. This
contains the overcoat and any spare clothes that
are carried. All this together, with one hundred
rounds of ammunition, is distinctly hefty. Add a
blanket and a ground sheet (waterproof), and the
whole thing must weigh at least sixty-five pounds.
The webbing equipment is, however, well arranged,
and distributes the weight about as well as could
be devised. The blanket and " wetter-sheet " are
worn rolled up like a bandolier."

After a day under canvas here the H.A.C. was
billeted in two school buildings, evidently only recently used by French recruits, as they found
French military phrases on the blackboards.

[LETTER]

September 27, 1914.

" The last two days we have been transferred
to various school buildings in place of under canvas. On the whole, this is an improvement. The
floors are a trifle harder, but it is not quite so cold
at night. To-day, Sunday, is the first slack day
since I joined. A bath is not permitted, as being
too expensive in water, but I have had as thorough
a wash as possible.

" Feeding arrangements have been better recently. Practically no leave is granted. Weather
is quite favourable, for which we are grateful."

[LETTER]

September 30, 1914.

"Your letter of September 20th reached me
to-day. Yes, in view of previous unfortunate experiences with the commissariat organisation I am
keeping my own private emergency rations on
hand, but things are better now, though rather
monotonous. I understand tobacco parcels can be
sent without duty, and I shall be glad to get them.
We have had a two-ounce packet of tobacco issued
to us, and are supposed to get it once a week. I
am also eking out with local baccy, which, however, is not much good. As to news, we get the
main features from a local paper.

" You will be interested to hear I have had my

first typhoid inoculation. It made me feel pretty groggy for twenty-four hours—chills and aches like ' flue '—but I am all right again now, barring a rather stiff shoulder (the stuff was shot in on the chest near the shoulder). Another dose in about ten days' time. Almost all of us had it done.

" After a false alarm of an immediate move a few days ago, we seem to be well settled for the present, and things are therefore not quite so rushed for us as they were. The pioneers' chief work comes when moving into new quarters.

" Being in a town we are now able to send little boys on errands for us (not being able to leave our quarters), and we are supplementing official dietary with eggs, fruit, etc."

About this time No. 2 Company went away, their destination, as was heard later, being Abbeville. The pioneers remained attached to the Headquarters Company, No. 1.

[LETTER]

October 4, 1914.

" Since writing you last a new regulation has been issued. We are now to write only one letter per week.

" We are still billeted in the school-house here, that is to say, some of us. Other parties have gone to various places on different jobs.

" I had some quite interesting work this week, being detailed as orderly (Anglicé messenger) to the supply depot at the station. There were two of us, one always to be within call. At night we slept on the platform within a few yards of the office. We slept on some sacks of oats—quite luxurious in comparison with board floors.

" It was quite interesting to see something of the life in the town and the handling of the supplies. There are comparatively few motor vehicles to be seen anywhere, and those that are here are nearly all English trucks—Carter Paterson, etc. A Kent County Council lorry was particularly active at the station ; also a W. and G. taxi. Various public buildings are occupied by different portions of our troops. For instance, one is used by the signal section of the Engineers as a telegraph office.

" We expect to be on the move again in a few days' time."

This job only lasted a few days, to the Mole's regret, as it gave him a considerable amount of freedom to get about while taking messages. He utilised the opportunity to go to the Bank of France to change the £1 notes he had with him into five-franc notes, that being the only place they were accepted. As time was short he went there in an open fiacre to the amusement of several of the H.A.C. men who saw him, and who chaffed him about being an orderly de luxe. It was, of course, somewhat irregular as, strictly speaking, he should have returned to the depot directly after

delivering the message.   The O.C. depot was a
grizzled old captain in the A.S.C., and quite un-
military, so it did not much matter.   This officer
seemed to be quite surprised on being saluted, and
all the finer points of H.A.C. smartness were quite
wasted on him.

Up to this time everyone was confined to their
billets unless detailed on some duty, but now it was
stated that an afternoon's leave would be granted
every ten days.   The most pressing matter that
everyone attended to when leave was available was
to get a bath, as in billets this was unobtainable.

[LETTER]

October 11, 1914.

" As to parcels I have come to the conclusion
that it would be best to register them if possible,
as some men have found theirs tampered with and
contents extracted.

" Quite a number of our men speak the
language, more or less.   I have not had much
opportunity of utilising my knowledge of it, as I
have had only three hours' leave since we landed,
though it has come in handy for sending boys on
errands to purchase things.   The weather is pretty
chilly when the sun goes down, but so far I have
all the clothing I require, as I provided for it as
much as possible.

" I cannot tell you where we are, but think I
may say we are not in the firing-line.   The work

has been quite interesting, and we have had some practice in advancing, covering advances, bayonet work, and the final charge. The idea is that as one section advances the remainder keep the enemy suppressed by means of rapid fire, and so afford protection. This is carried out until all are in line again, and finally within a short distance of the enemy trenches, when the bayonet is fixed (still lying flat on the ground), and the whole force charges forward as hard as it can go, cheering with what breath may be left!

" We are still at the school, but expect to move at short notice. The second inoculation was to have commenced but has been postponed for the present."

Evidently the Mole evaded the regulation as to only one letter per week, for he writes again :—

October, 13. 1914.

" Almost immediately after sending off my last letter I was very pleased to have the first two of my parcels arrive and *intact*. I may interpolate here that the procedure of sending letters is somewhat devious. First, via the hands of the section sergeant, who collects them and hands them to an officer who censors and initials the envelope. What happens after that I am not sure, but I believe they are taken to the post office where they are inspected for the officer's signature.

" The cigarettes have been chiefly distributed amongst my friends and have been greatly appreciated. To most of the men English cigarettes are a great prize. All of it was corn in Egypt, especially after the disquieting rumours of parcels being raided by the Army Service Corps en route. Some of the others are getting cigarettes sent out, but none had so far arrived, so we were all feeling very uneasy about parcels, and the arrival of mine has revived hopes.

" We get our pay, 1s. per day, in French money once a week. That is, it is supposed to be French, but it is quite a jumble of Swiss, Belgian or even Italian silver. However, it can all be disposed of, if not at the first place, then somewhere else. It comes in quite useful for adding to funds on hand, though I am still quite decently supplied.

" We had quite a little excitement the other day. A man was seen wearing a mixed French uniform and English equipment. An armed party was sent out after him to investigate as it was thought he might be a German spy attempting disguise. I believe eventually it turned out after he was brought in that he had bought the stuff from some Tommy, and, as far as we know, nothing further happened.

" I have now had and recovered from my second inoculation, after about the same procedure as before.

" I should certainly like to apply for a commission if there is any chance of getting one, as it looks to me as if the supply of officers will be our most pressing need in view of all the new troops being raised. I believe, however, that there are already thousands of applications in and do not know how being on active service would affect this. If Major D. can do anything it would be quite agreeable to me.

" We have seen some of the London Scottish. Like ourselves, they are split up into various parties, doing work in different parts. They seem to come in for a large amount of writing up, which we characterise as twaddle or rude words to that effect.

" I forgot to say that I have sent up one hundred cigarettes to the English in the hospital to be distributed by our medical orderlies. They won't go far, but even so will be welcome."

[LETTER FROM MAJOR D., D.S.O., TO H. G.]

Grantham, October 19, 1914.

" Before replying to your letter I showed it to my General, who agreed with the opinion I had already formed. If your son had not already been serving my General could have got him a commission without any difficulty; but the fact that he is serving already makes it very difficult, especially as he is on active service.

" Owing to the fact that he is serving any

recommendation for a commission must come from his own Commanding Officer, and, therefore, the best thing for him to do is to apply to his Commanding Officer to forward his name for a commission in the New Army.

" It is very bad luck that his keenness in serving as a private should have created a difficulty in his obtaining a commission, but I am sure you will understand that when once a man is serving his name can only be put forward by his own superior officer.

" The news now seems very satisfactory. Lord Kitchener was here yesterday and he seemed very confident."

Major D.'s Brigade afterwards went to Gallipoli.

[LETTER]
October 18, 1914.

" I seem to have got out of the typhoid inoculation very well on the whole, as I practically had recovered after twenty-four hours, while a number of men were knocked over for the best part of a week. However, as it is supposed to protect you for about two years it is worth the temporary rotten feeling it causes.

" After the process of scattering mentioned in previous letters we now have here only one company, headquarters staff and attachments (pioneers, signallers, machine-guns, etc.). The men here have been occupied with drilling, route marches, bayonet practice and field exercises, providing guards for the railway, supplies depot, orderlies for the Base headquarters office, etc. Through the comparatively prolonged stay in one place my special work has slackened off, so that I have been able to get my share of most of this.

" There is no regular schedule for the day as the programme depends altogether on what there is in hand, but we are up at six and kept pretty well occupied until evening. The life in a way is quite interesting, though some things get very monotonous. The inevitable stew for dinner, while of good material and ample quantity, becomes tiresome. It seems to be the only thing that can be cooked in large quantities on a camp fire.

" Breakfast has been the least satisfactory meal, as large quantities of bacon issued were unfit for consumption. For some time we had none at all, and after that a very short ration. It is only within the last few days that we have had what we were entitled to. The official jam ration is a very small one. Of course, this does not mean that we do not fare pretty well, as we supplement official dietary with outside purchases.

" Another feature of daily life that is a particular nuisance is cleaning one's feeding utensils after each meal, and some men make a very hasty

job of it.   Probably a good housewife would have
a fit over the results achieved.''

About this time the Mole decided that to facili-
tate matters he would purchase an enamelled dish
as being more convenient than the official mess-
tin ; he already had an enamelled mug.   This ware
could be readily washed out under a tap, and had
no awkward corners.   The bottom of the dish being
brown was suitable for strapping on to the haversack.

[THE LETTER CONTINUES]

" I am sleeping quite well, but it means turning
over a good deal in the night, the reason being that
on a flat surface like the floor, with nothing under
you but a thin ' wetter ' sheet, most of the weight
of the body comes on the hip-bone, and you cannot
lie for very long on one side.   Taking it all round,
we are better off in the building than under canvas,
and I should hope that, whatever our future move
may be, we shall not be camped out again until it
becomes a necessity in the field.

" In some ways I think it has been a good
thing to bring us over here.   The stricter discipline
and feeling of responsibility that must be impressed
on even the youngsters of the company when
actually on service should be beneficial.   On the
other hand, field exercises are much interrupted and
rifle practice discontinued.   It is in this last respect that some of our men are rather deficient.

Indeed, if it were not for my own previous rifle shooting, I should feel distinctly uncomfortable about it, as owing to other work I have had very little opportunity.

"I should judge that the English papers publish the bulk of the news several days earlier than the local ones here. We sometimes get hold of a Paris *Daily Mail*, and find it fully a day ahead of the others.

"Judging by one or two fur coats I have seen, I should say it gets very cold here in the winter. Our own coats are quite good, but of course only of cloth. They are grey (like the Guards'), and we have wondered if we might not be mistaken for Germans. We understand that khaki ones are to be substituted shortly to conform with the uniform and the rest of the troops.

"The life of this town seems to be proceeding much as usual. Of course, it has the ubiquitous Place de la République with surrounding cafés. One sees about the same number of people sipping at the little tables outside. There are lots of soldiers about still, but that might be accounted for by the supposition that it was a garrison town. The incongruous note is struck by the khaki uniforms one sees all over the place. What it is like after dark I do not know, as our leave (when we get it) only runs from 4 to 7. The type of local soldier one sees is not very impressive, but I suppose every efficient man of their own Army has long ago gone to the Front. Quite a number of detachments of our Regulars are located here.

"In view of the colder weather we were delighted to have a second blanket served out to us. This is a great improvement, though just what will happen when we move off I do not know. It would be a very heavy burden if it has to be carried.

"We are fortunate in having gas in the building (only our own candles everywhere else up to now), so that we can read or write in the evenings, a good deal of card-playing also going on. We turn in pretty early—'lights out' at 10 P.M. I think I explained before that going to bed is quite an elaborate affair. It involves putting on practically as much fresh clothing as you take off in order to keep warm (provided you are not expecting marching orders, in which case you simply lie down as you are). It is simple enough here, where there is plenty of room, but in a bell tent, with, say, twelve or more occupants, there is so little room that only one man can move at a time. The first time we experienced it it was like a pantomime rehearsal, and though we were all soaked and miserable, we ended up with shrieks of laughter. Taking things as they come, we manage to extract some fun out of our experiences.

"I enclose some photographs, the best a local man could do in a hurry."

The detachment of the H.A.C. still remaining at Le Mans was now chiefly engaged at the ordnance depot called Maroc, i.e. Morocco (presumably from being situated on a sandy waste a few miles out of town). It appeared to have been designed as a huge goods clearing station, only just nearing completion, and with its long sheds and railway tracks was well adapted as a storage centre from which supplies could be forwarded.

The Mole was much impressed with the systematic way supplies were marked. All boxes, &c., had a coloured band painted round them indicating that they were for the advance base depot, and appeared to have been in ordnance store in England all ready for sending to an expeditionary force. All cases, &c., were well made and adapted for shipment, and he felt that, for its size, the British Expeditionary Force was very well organised and equipped, everything having been thought out and prepared beforehand. As we know, this Army was shipped to the Continent without a hitch in a way that betokened literally perfect organisation. As for the Army itself, though only small by modern standards, it was the finest weapon of war that has ever been forged. There has never been anything to compare with it.

[LETTER]
October 23, 1914.

" You will in the meantime have seen that

letters and parcels are coming through all right, though sometimes delayed. The air cushion has proved very useful, though I am putting it to a different use to what I originally intended. I am putting it under my hip, as I have got quite used to a kit-bag as a pillow, in spite of sundry boot-heels, &c., forming hard lumps in it.

"The men here are all congenial, though I have not so far become particularly chummy with any one man in particular.

"I think it was scandalous the way they sent the untrained and ill-equipped Naval Division to Antwerp. Judging by what I saw of their unprepared condition at Deal, I can quite believe the description given in the letter to the *Times* on that subject.

"Our work has been quite varied of late, mostly out at the base ordnance depot, loading and unloading trains, sorting supplies, &c. Amongst other things we have had to strip a lot of equipment returned from the front, much of it shot to pieces and some of it in a pretty ghastly condition. All the serviceable stuff is sorted out for use again. I forgot to say that some of our men have been guarding and escorting German prisoners, convoying supply trains, &c.

"We are still in our schoolhouse, but hear rumours of a move from time to time. Quite an event of the week was an opportunity to get a hot bath when I was out on leave.

" I note the correspondence with Major **D.** (re commission) with interest. We must see what comes of it. With regard to the restriction of the number of letters sent, we are told that the restriction was not so much imposed to lighten the work of the censoring officer as to relieve the congestion of mail, and so allow the postal service to expedite letters from the Front.

" You have probably seen the enclosed cutting from the dispatch of French (re advance base), but I send it in case it escaped your attention."

This last was a broad hint as to the locality of the writer, which was understood.

August had been a month of blazing heat, and the fine weather extended for the greater part of September, but by now—the latter part of October—it began to turn cold, though still mostly dry. This cold, though not yet by any means severe, made itself felt, as there was no means of heating the billets, nor was this ever possible even later on in the worst winter months, which turned out to be the wettest on record for many years. Cooking was done in a primitive fashion over camp fires of wood in the yard. The supply of wood was not too plentiful, and there was always a certain amount of squabbling when drawing the daily ration, each party trying to get a maximum allotment. In consequence of this the gentle art of "pinching" was exercised when opportunity offered.

In these early days of the war, when men started their active service and might be rushed to the firing line almost immediately, the polishing of buttons ceased as soon as they embarked. Men had to be got over the strip of water at top speed, and the mobilisation stores were hard put to it to find boots, ankle, let alone such trifles as brushes, brass, or any of those little tins which greeted the 1916 citizen soldier the day after his arrival at the depot. The Mole rejoiced when his buttons took on a gun-metal hue and the colour of his cap-badge invited comparison with the bronze of the officers' badge.

Conditions were all rough-and-ready. Ablutions had to be performed with a bucket of water, one bucket to about twenty men, so the general scramble can be imagined. One of the standard jokes of the time was to write home saying : "For washing we use a bucket of water ; when the bugle sounds we fall in!" As a matter of fact there were no bugles nor any bands. Orders were supposed to be given by whistle signals in the field, but actually commands were always given by word of mouth.

Like all the troops, the **H.A.C.** amused themselves with singing, particularly on the march. The prime favourite was a Rabelaisian ballad detailing the many adventures of "Frolicky Bill

the Sailor "; a close second was a much amended
version of the Mother Goose nursery rhymes,
winding up with the chorus :

" Hurrah for little Mary, hurrah for the lamb,
  Hurrah for the teacher who did not care a little
    bit ;
  And everywhere that Mary went the lamb was
    sure to go,
  Shouting out the battle-cry of freedom."

In view of what the Mole had now been informed as to obtaining a commission, he decided
to approach the C.O., but his application was
curtly rejected. With the recommendation of his
C.O. he could have obtained a commission through
Major D.

Friday, October 30.—After many rumours of
impending movement, definite orders were at last
issued to pack up and move off. Kit-bags were
handed over to the tender mercies of the transport again, billets were given a final clean up, and
all regimental baggage was loaded. At the last
moment these orders were cancelled. This led to
a funny incident. The " Gorringe " cart had
been loaded with a miscellaneous collection of stuff
which was quite heavy. One of the transport men
was holding up the shafts so that the horse could
be unharnessed and led away. As soon as the
horse was withdrawn from the shafts the weight
of the cart shot them up in the air, and the trans-

port man was so astonished that he clung to the shafts and was shot up too!

Owing to the sudden change of plan the ration supply was again deficient, and in order to help matters a number of men were granted a few hours' leave (by lot) so that they could feed themselves, the rations to be divided amongst the less fortunate remainder.

Saturday, October 31.—The detachment left Le Mans at 9.30 A.M., and arrived at Rouen at midnight; then proceeded via Boulogne and Calais. Destination unknown. The other companies rejoined at various points, so that the H.A.C. again formed a battalion.

CHAPTER VI

THE EARLY MONTHS OF THE WAR

No attempt will be made here to give more than a sketchy outline of the events during the first few months of the war. More qualified writers have dealt fully with this subject, and readers desirous of more detail should turn to " The First Seven Divisions," by Hamilton. It is, however, necessary to mention the salient features in order to bring the movements of the H.A.C. into the perspective of the general progress of events.

On Sunday, August 23rd, the first clash of the British and German Armies took place at Mons. The enemy attacked in great strength with a simultaneous concentration of a hitherto unheard of artillery fire. Equally unprecedented was the efficient direction of this bombardment by aeroplanes, rendering it exceedingly accurate and destructive. Nevertheless, out-manned and out-gunned as they were, their ranks shattered and a large proportion of their batteries put out of action, the British forces held the line, only withdrawing slightly from a dangerous salient. On Sunday night Sir John French was astounded to hear of the retirement of the French troops on his right. This rendered the Mons line untenable, and orders were given to the British troops to fall back. The *Retreat from Mons* had begun.

With regard to the battle itself a silly legend became current that angels had been seen fighting in and among the sadly thinned ranks of our men to stem the tide of the German onrush. As one survivor aptly commented : " If the angels were on our side at Mons, I hope the next time they will help the Germans."

The British Army fell back, making successive stands at Valenciennes — Maubeuge (August 24th); Cambrai—Le Cateau—Landrecies (August 25th); Le Catelet (August 26th); Ham, south of St. Quentin (August 27th), and Noyon (August 28th).

French writes in his dispatch of September 7th of " the most critical day of all, viz., the 26th : At daybreak it became apparent that the enemy was throwing the bulk of his strength against the left of the position occupied by the Second Corps and the 4th Division.

" At this time the guns of four German army corps were in position against them, and Sir Horace Smith-Dorrien reported to me that he judged it impossible to continue his retirement at daybreak (as ordered) in face of such an attack. I sent him orders to use his utmost endeavours to break off the action and retire at the earliest possible moment, as it was impossible for me to send him any support.

" The French Cavalry Corps, under General Sordet, was coming up on our left rear early in the morning, and I sent him an urgent message to do his utmost to come up and support the retirement of my left flank; but owing to the fatigue of his horses he found himself unable to intervene in any way.

" There had been no time to entrench the position properly, but the troops showed a magnificent front to the terrible fire which confronted them. The artillery, although outmatched by at least four to one, made a splendid fight and inflicted heavy losses on their opponents.

" At length it became apparent that if complete annihilation were to be avoided a retirement must be attempted, and the order was given to commence it at 3.30 P.M.

" Fortunately, the enemy had himself suffered too heavily to engage in an energetic pursuit."

This retreat was continued far into the night of the 26th and through the 27th and 28th. The men were exhausted with constant marching 25 and 30 miles a day, stopping only for a few hours' rest or a rearguard action. Units became broken up, snatching what rest they could by the side of the road. The weather was blazing hot, and men threw away their coats and packs to lighten the load, retaining little more than their rifles. The Germans were always hot on their heels, and there seems to be reason for believing that they were brought forward in innumerable motor-lorries.

To those in command and cognisant of the situation it looked almost desperate.

Frederic Coleman writes in his book, " Mons to Ypres " : " For a time I was to act as usher at a point a bit north of St. Quentin. Never shall I forget the staff-officer's parting instructions : ' Cheer them up as you keep them on the move. No wonder they are tired ! Worn out to begin with, then fighting all day—no rest, no food, no sleep—poor devils. Tell them where to go and cheer them up.' I had not been long on that roadside when I realised that many of us had been labouring under a great delusion. It was not that someone was needed to cheer up Tommy; it was that most of us needed Tommy to cheer *us* up."

French concludes his dispatch on the battle up to this point : " I deeply deplore the very serious losses which the British forces have suffered in this great battle, but they were inevitable in view of the fact that the British Army—only two days after a concentration by rail—was called upon to withstand a vigorous attack of five German army corps."

At last, on August 28th, the British had thrown off the weight of the enemy's pursuit, and our forces, reduced to nearly half their original strength, had some opportunity to re-form ; but further retirement was still necessary, and in conformity with the movements of the French forces was continued practically from day to day.

Although not severely pressed by the enemy, rearguard actions took place continually.

Finally, on Saturday, September 5th, the enemy had crossed the Marne, and their advanced troops were only about thirty miles from Paris. Joffre then announced his intention to take the offensive forthwith, and there ensued the *Battle of the Marne*, probably the most decisive engagement and the turning-point of the whole war. The Germans appeared to be within reach of their goal when Foch in a brilliant action pierced their line and so forced their retreat.

French reports this battle in his dispatch of September 17th : " On that day " (September 6th) " it may be said that a great battle opened on a front extending from Ermenonville to a point north of the fortress of Verdun. This battle may be said to have concluded on the evening of September 10th, by which time the Germans had been driven back to the line Soissons—Rheims with a loss of thousands of prisoners, many guns, and enormous masses of transport.

" In concluding this dispatch I must call your Lordships' special attention to the fact that from Sunday, August 23rd, up to the present date (September 17th), from Mons back almost to the Seine, my command has been ceaselessly engaged without one single day's halt or rest of any kind."

By the night of September 12th the enemy had arrested his retreat, and was preparing to dispute the line of the Aisne. On the morning of September 13th French ordered the British forces to advance and make good the passage of the river. In this manner the *Battle of the Aisne* commenced. On the left the leading troops reached the river by 9 o'clock. They were only enabled to cross in single file and under considerable shell-fire by means of a broken girder of a bridge which was not entirely submerged. A pontoon bridge was constructed later. Similar crossings were effected at other points. In the evening the enemy retired at all points, and entrenched himself on the high ground along which runs the Chemin-des-Dames. This position was only captured by the French in 1917.

Up to this time there was every hope that the continued retirement of the enemy would be enforced. By the morning of the 15th it became clear that the enemy was making a determined stand, though little our men thought that the enemy position would be maintained for the best part of three years! It is a striking commentary on the thoroughness of the German Staff that, although they must have been practically certain of the success of the coup against Paris, tney had nevertheless prepared these positions against the almost inconceivable chance of a miscarriage of their plan.

The battle lasted until September 28th. Time and again the British troops attacked, only to be repulsed with great loss by withering artillery fire. The arrival of the 6th Division was a much needed and welcome addition to their depleted strength. The enemy, on his side, launched a number of counter-attacks, but without success. The severe tax on the endurance of the troops was increased by the heavy rain and cold which prevailed for some ten or twelve days of this trying time, particularly as the men were now destitute of adequate clothing.

Trench warfare had now begun. Once it was realised that the Germans were firmly established in their selected defensive positions on the Aisne, the next development was a race between the opposing armies for the Channel ports, hitherto practically abandoned by the Allies and neglected by the Germans, each side extending its line northward in the vain endeavour to outflank the other.

French describes this struggle, culminating in the *First Battle of Ypres*, in his dispatch dated November 20th, 1914 : " Early in October a study of the general situation strongly impressed me with the necessity of bringing the greatest possible force to bear in support of the northern flank of the Allies in order effectively to outflank the enemy and compel him to evacuate his positions.

" Arrangements for withdrawal and relief having been made by the French General Staff, the operation commenced on October 3rd, and the

move was completed on October 19th, when the
First Corps under Sir Douglas Haig completed its
detrainment at St. Omer.

British troops were in the meantime already in
action, commencing October 11th near Bethune.
Bailleul was taken on the 14th, and by the 17th,
with the co-operation of the French, the enemy
was driven back beyond Ypres. The British Army
was now reinforced by Rawlinson's troops (3rd
Cavalry Division and the 7th Division), which had
previously been sent to Antwerp. The remnant
of the Belgian Army was rendering what assistance it could by entrenching themselves on the
Ypres Canal and the Yser River. On the 21st the
British were still on the offensive, and attempted
to take Passchendaele. It was arranged that the
French should hand over Ypres to the British and
cover their left flank.

The Germans were by this time (October 23rd)
strongly reinforced, and took the offensive, the
Allies suffering severely under their attacks. The
British forces were extended from Ypres to Arras
and the line was only thinly held. The Germans
launched one attack after another, the British
counter-attacking when opportunity offered, but
being gradually forced to retire. An order taken
from a German prisoner showed that the Kaiser
had ordered the German army to break through
the line to Ypres as the gate to Calais. Their
most important and decisive attack (except that

of the Prussian Guard on November 15th) was on
October 31st. The situation was critical, and was
only saved by a desperate counter-attack accom-
plishing the recapture of Gheluvelt. French writes
that " this was fraught with momentous consequences. If any one unit can be singled out for
especial praise, it is the Worcesters."

To the London Scottish was assigned an
important part in maintaining the Messines Ridge.
They fought gallantly, but under overwhelming
attacks they were driven back on Sunday, November 1st. The ridge was gone, Wytschaete captured
by the enemy, and Messines had to be abandoned.

The Indian troops had now arrived and played
their part in the great struggle, which began to
die down by November 20th.

The outstanding feature of the British Army
was its effective rifle-fire. Machine-guns were few,
but the men of the original Expeditionary Force
had been trained for years in rapid and accurate
shooting, and no living thing could face a burst
of fifteen rounds rapid in the " mad minute " of
fire. So deadly was this fire that it was long before
the German would believe that our forces were
not plentifully supplied with machine-guns, as they
were themselves. Under this destructive fire the
advancing ranks of the Germans were mown down
in swathes.

The following is extracted from Coleman's

description of the battle and the attack of the Prussian Guard in particular :

" The enemy's plan of attack never varied. His guns shelled hard, preparing the way for his, infantry, massed, often deeply, on a narrow front. Battalion came behind battalion, regiment behind regiment. The foremost body repulsed, the reserve stepped into the breach and continued the attack. Should the first attempt prove successful and a foothold be gained, reserves were brought up without delay to hold and, if possible, to widen the breach in the line.

" Hurling back the initial attack and pounding to atoms each front line that pressed on was of vital importance. Every foothold had to be torn loose at no matter what bloody cost. No limit bounded the endurance and the effectiveness of the British soldier save death itself. The impossible was achieved so often in front of Ypres that its performance ceased to cause wonder and hardly attracted attention. No explanation will ever be forthcoming as to why the Germans did not win through to Ypres. Time after time they won a hole in the line, blocked by no reserves, because there were none. Companies faced brigades of the advancing enemy, and somehow held them off. Never had so much killing been done. The dead seemed to outnumber the living. Yet the line held in some way. It was beyond comprehension.

" The Prussian Guard had come on as if on

parade ; whole regiments had withered away under
a stream of fire, and others relentlessly advanced
over their dead bodies as if unmindful of their own
certain fate.   A gunner told me that one battalion
of Prussians had broken through our line and
marched straight towards our guns.   Coming
within one hundred yards of his battery, they had
been literally blown back, leaving their dead in
ghastly heaps to mark the limit of their bold
advance."

The Kaiser's orders had cost him the flower of
his army.   And so the opposing lines settled down
to trench warfare.   French concludes his report
(dated November 20th) of the battle : " In the
period covered by this dispatch Territorial troops
have been used for the first time in the army under
my command.

" The units actually engaged have been the
Northumberland, Northamptonshire, North Somer-
set, Leicestershire and Oxfordshire Regiments of
Yeomanry Cavalry ; and the London Scottish,
Hertfordshire, Honourable Artillery Company
and Queen's Westminster Battalions of Territorial
Infantry.

" The conduct and bearing of these units under
fire and the efficient manner in which they carried
out the various duties assigned to them have
imbued me with the highest hope as to the value
and help of Territorial troops generally."

CHAPTER VII

FLANDERS

Sunday, November 1.—The H.A.C. arrived at St. Omer at 9 P.M., tired with their cramped journey, and marched to their billets in the old French barracks on the farther edge of the town. Until their arrival they had no idea where they were or what was in store for them. Many believed that on detraining they would march straight to the firing-line, or, as they said, " We're for it! " The first news that greeted them was a report that the London Scottish had been surrounded by the enemy and had been wiped out. Fortunately this was a much exaggerated report. It was soon learned that Sir John French was making his headquarters in the town.

Monday, November 2.—Khaki overcoats were served out in place of their original ones. The men had one last opportunity to get at their kitbags before parting with them for good. The bags disappeared into the unknown, and, as was afterwards heard, were sent to Armoury House, whence they could be recovered.

Tuesday, November 3.—Detachments were instructed to dig trenches about four miles out of St. Omer. It was never quite clear whether this was for purposes of instruction or for the possible defence of the town—perhaps for both.

Wednesday, November 4.—None of the men had ever fired the particular model of rifle which had last been issued to them, so they were all pleased to be given a chance to test them on the local range. Barrels were now cleaned out, in some cases not a simple process, as they were plugged tight with hard grease, and each man fired five rounds, not always with brilliant results.

Thursday, November 5.—The battalion left St. Omer at 9 A.M., riding in motor-buses. Rumour gave the destination as Bailleul, and for once proved to be correct. En route they ascended the steep hill on which Cassel is situated, an outstanding eminence in a generally flat country.

[LETTER]

"*November* 6, 1914.

"We have been so much on the move and so busy that there has been no opportunity of writing. Since my last letter we have had a two days' train journey to General Headquarters, and thence per L.G.O. bus on to the little town where we are now billeted. Amongst other things, we have had route marching, trench digging (for possible defence purposes) and firing practice. In short we have been so busy, from the first thing in the morning to 'lights out,' that there has hardly been a moment to spare. We have now parted with our kit-bags for good, and our second blanket has also been given up. For the present we retain one, but I should not be surprised if we also gave that up.

"The journey here reminded one of the old ' dog-Latin ' joke : Is ab ille heres ago fortibus es in aro—I say, Billy, here's a go ; forty buses in a row. The amount of motor transport over here must be something enormous, and I should think the English are far ahead of anyone else in that respect."

Saturday, *November* 7.—The H.A.C. marched at night to Estaires, about thirteen miles S.E. of Bailleul and S.W. of Armentières. Oh, those night marches! The roads consisted of a narrow strip of pavé bordered by mud, which in many places was one or two feet deep, and moving to one side to overtake or allow troops or vehicles to pass meant stepping into a sea of liquid slush. The cobbles were bad and ankle-twisting, so that it made marching difficult. At short intervals the line would halt suddenly without warning, to immediately start forward again, and perhaps in a moment's time blocked again by other regiments on the road. The men were not used to the weight of the pack, and the slings cut painfully into their shoulders. A march like this seemed interminable. No one knew where they were or how far they still had to go. The wet weather set in now in earnest, and more often than not it was pouring in torrents. Footsore, their nerves rasped by the frequent checks which made the rate of progression exceedingly slow, their shoulders galled by the pack, the ragged ranks cursed and stumbled blindly forward in the pitch-black of a wet winter's night. From time to time a halt of a few minutes would be called, and the exhausted men flung themselves down anywhere in the middle of the road for a brief respite. Later the roads grew so bad that systematic work of repairing them had to be undertaken. The sides were filled in with corduroy, logs of timber placed side by side, and surfaced with broken brick where available (from shelled houses). Bricks were also used for repairing shell holes in the road.

The battalion stayed at Estaires the next day, many of them being billeted in a girls' school (unoccupied).

Monday, November 9.—The next march was to La Couture, near Bethune. Here the H.A.C. were for the first time billeted in various farm-houses. These proved to be typical of Northern France and Flanders. The farm buildings are set in a square about an open space, the dwelling house forming one side of the square, barns, stables, outhouses, &c., forming the remaining three sides. In the centre, bordered by a narrow walk all round about four feet wide, is a large open pit. This is filled with an odoriferous collection of manure and all the refuse of the farm. Woe betide the hapless wight who in the inky darkness

misses the strait and narrow path and stumbles
into the ungodly mess!

The officers usually found billets in the dwelling house, other ranks in the barns, &c., but ever
invading the kitchen to drink coffee, which
Madame was always only too pleased to supply
for a few sous. Here Grandpa was always to be
found, smoking tobacco that overflowed the bowl
of his pipe in a curious way, but quite ready to
accept some ration navy cut.

There also was the first experience just behind
the firing-line, and detachments were detailed for
digging new trenches. Where or what they were
the Mole never learned, but they were, presumably, reserve trenches between Armentières and
Arras. They were subjected to spasmodic shelling, and on the night of November 13-14th two
men were killed, the first casualties. They were
buried in one of the little gardens of the village.

The following is an extract published in the
Daily Telegraph from a letter dated November
14th of another member of the H.A.C. :

" Have had a very busy week—no time to write
a line. Up at six, off before dawn, digging
trenches near the firing-line; back at dark.
Weather horrid. We are billeted in a beastly
barn, into which rain and wind blows, but we
manage to keep well. It is most interesting here.

" I have had my first experience of fire. It is
not at all alarming; no casualties. We acted as

reserves. The Germans are thoroughly demoralised, and their fire is nothing to be frightened at. They have been shelling our trenches for some time without damage until yesterday, when, unfortunately, we sustained our first loss—nine casualties."

The following is an extract from a letter of another member of the H.A.C. published in the " British Westinghouse Club News " :

" *November* 17, 1914.

" We are now having a day or perhaps two days' rest after a strenuous ten days in Well, you have to guess. You may be assisted if I say we are covered from head to foot with clay. You should see us now, after having been wet through with rain, snow and sleet, not washed nor shaved for ten days, no clothes off for about sixteen days. We live on bully beef and biscuits. It's the discomforts, I say, that are the hardest side of war. Even when you do get a chance to take boots off, we dare not, as we might never get them on again. But we are still alive—very much so.

" I am not even allowed to put any official address on this, in case it falls into enemy's hands. We don't want them to know what regiments they have against them, for, as you will have seen by the home papers, they find out the officers' names from, I suppose, our Army List, then shout out to us : ' Major So-and-so says retire ! ' If you do,

they pot you in the process severely. My equipment is now boiled down to the absolute minimum.
You know the packs on our backs. Well, mine
includes a sleeping helmet, pair of gauntlets, half
a pound of tobacco, two hundred cigarettes, one
pair of socks, handkerchief, maps. Not much, you
say, but every ounce tells on a long march in bad
country, with food, greatcoat, and two hundred
rounds of ammunition. Sometimes I wish I were
in the cavalry, as a horse carries the lot.''

On Sunday, November 15th, the first fall of
snow was experienced. This was the critical day
when, some miles to the north, the Prussian Guard
nearly broke through to Ypres, though the H.A.C.
were wholly unaware of the progress of events.
They were always dependent on newspapers from
England for information as to what was happening outside their own narrow horizon. Rumours,
mostly unfounded, flourished as ever. One that
cropped up from time to time, always "just
reported by the divisional signallers" or some
such infallible authority, related to a tremendous
battle in the North Sea : " The flagship, the *Iron
Duke*, was sunk, but the German Fleet was completely destroyed.''

The weather was now turning very cold. The
Mole found the question of clothing something of
a problem; if too ample it meant profuse perspiration on the march, while however much one piled

on it was cold when not on the move, bad enough
in the unheated and draughty billets, and bitter
in the trench. He compromised by wearing under
his tunic heavy underwear, a flannel shirt and two
thin cardigan jackets for marching; in his pack he
had an additional thick woolly sweater, which he
put on when opportunity offered on arrival at the
trench. In billets, for greater ease, he substituted
the " woolly " for his tunic, which he used as a
pillow. With a " wetter " sheet spread out to lie
on, and rolled up in a blanket with the overcoat
on top, this was comparative comfort. This and
the removal of boots, and sometimes, as a great
luxury, a change of socks, constituted the *toilette
de nuit.*

Before leaving this part of the line the battalion was inspected by Sir James Willcocks, who
used what seems to be stereotyped phraseology,
congratulating the C.O. on his " fine body of
men." Willcocks was in command of the Indian
Corps, to which the H.A.C. were, presumably,
attached for the time being, as was also the case
with certain other British units.

Monday, November 16.—Orders were suddenly
given to move off, and the H.A.C. marched back
to Bailleul, or, as the Tommies all called it,
" Belloo." Here the battalion rested the next
four days. They probably constituted part of the
reserve, as they were hardly allowed to leave their
billets and might have been called on at any

moment. However, the rest was necessary.
Hardly a man had a whole pair of boots, and a
plentiful supply had to be issued. About this time
attention was forcibly drawn to another matter.
Numbers of the men reported to the medical officer
with an unfamiliar irritation of the skin. The
diagnosis by the M.O. was " Lice," no doubt
from the various filthy billets. Beautiful theoreti-
cal advice was given as to how to get rid of them
by virtually starving them out, i.e. by a change of
shirt and underwear for a week, but as no one
was physically able to get any change of clothing
other than a pair or two of socks into his pack,
already filled with an assortment of necessary odd-
ments, this was of no avail. The only palliative
was to go on the hunt from time to time as opportunity offered. It may here be noted that at no
time did anyone have an extra uniform, and since
leaving St. Omer each man had practically just
what he stood up in, wet or dry, day or night.

Saturday, November 21. — The battalion
marched across the Belgian frontier to Neuve
Eglise, making headquarters there for practically
a week, detachments being detailed in turn to the
trenches. On the morning of their departure from
Bailleul they were paraded for an inspection by
Sir Horace Smith-Dorrien, who afterwards ad-
dressed them. Most of his speech was inaudible,
but he was understood to say that the main virtue
required at that time was endurance. He also gave

some encouragement as to the high percentage of
" dud " shells fired by the Germans, a statement
which, as far as the Mole's experience is concerned,
was never confirmed. Quite according to the War
Office sealed pattern, he concluded with a compli-
ment to the " fine body of men."

This phrase was later included in the H.A.C.
Golden Alphabet :

" B for battalion—fine body of men,
They once volunteered, but never again ! "

Letter from another member of the H.A.C.
(*The Times*) :

" *November* 25.

" We are right there now, and a real fighting
unit. Before we left the little town from which
I last wrote General —— made us a speech,
welcomed us to the firing-line, and told us our
present job was to hold the enemy—with various
encouragements and exhortations. Nowadays, as
it is mostly freezing, thirty-six or forty-eight hours
in the trenches are as much as one can do at a
time. We lie in this little townlet, just within
reach of the trenches, and but so far seldom shelled,
and go out a company at a time. On Sunday evening we started off, marched down the hill in the
dark, passed through a village which was being
shelled, and safely reached the reserve trenches.
There we stayed till close on dawn, when we moved
up to the firing trenches to relieve some Regulars.

Our trench consisted of four or five little 'dug-outs' (holes in which two or three can curl themselves up) connected by narrow trenches. During Monday morning we had a terrible time —we've had our baptism, but this was a deluge. The enemy's big guns had the range of our trench, and we lay very low for an hour or so, listening first to four dull bangs, then the long-drawn-out noise of an approaching shell, then a sickening pause and a tremendous explosion, followed by showers of earth and iron falling, sometimes by the smell of the explosive. Though not one of us was damaged, we found four full-fledged Jack Johnson holes within a radius of fifteen yards of us. Our platoon officer stood in one after dark, and his shoulders were on the level of my feet as I stood at the edge. Of course they aren't like shrapnel—they must hit you to hurt you, and it would be bad luck indeed if one's little hole in the earth were found by a gun miles away; but all the same one must admit that to anyone with the least imagination the first dose of it is a terrible thing. Next time it will be better, no doubt; very soon we shall be used to it. As a game it is beginning to get interesting, this fighting, but the horror of it and the continual sense of what Wells calls its 'd——d foolishness' I shall never get rid of.''

The writer of the above makes a mistake, no doubt due to inexperience. The shells referred to were probably 6-inch or, at the most, 8-inch. Quite bad enough, but the real Jack Johnson was 17-inch, and made a hole big enough to take a medium-sized house. Owing to the difficulty of moving it, the 17-inch howitzer was rarely shifted, and the Mole only saw it used against Ypres.

The correspondent in the " British Westinghouse Club News," already quoted, writes further :

" *November* 23, 1914.

" After four days at —— we marched on to where we are now. We no sooner got here than we marched off again to the trenches. The country is quite devastated, every farm and cottage one mass of ruins.

" The Germans started shelling our trench at daybreak. It was hellish while it lasted. We burrowed ' funk holes ' in the trenches, and they all caved in on us. About ten o'clock at night they started an attack on us. A roll of rifle-fire and machine-guns started up from the left until we were in it. The Germans absolutely poured lead into our trenches, and the machine-guns were buzzing away like sewing machines. We fired away at them like blazes and beat off their attack ; it lasted for about half an hour.

" You could fire back, whereas you can't at a shell. By the way, it was fearfully cold ; we were wet through, and then it froze, and our clothes got stiff. Worst part is cold feet."

The two following letters, written by members of the H.A.C., are extracted from *The Times*:

" Well, after doing work all over one country, we find ourselves in another, and with every prospect of having a very hot time, which is what we have all been praying for. At the last place but two we were at we were taking a second line of trenches and came in for some very hot fire. The next day they caught us as we were to take in slightly more advanced trenches, and we lay in a small ditch for about three hours with shell and rifle bullets jumping about over our heads and flicking leaves off the stunted willow trees in our ditch. One was quite safe and rather bored, as it poured with rain. I played a game of picquet with the man next me, and won two francs, then the rain stuck the cards together.

" The night before last we left at about five. It was quite pitch black and intensely cold, and snow lay heavily everywhere on fields, roofs and trees as we marched silently through the village and out into a long, long road with a wonderful avenue of trees, like Hobbema's famous picture at the National Gallery. On we go, hardly able to keep our footing on the frozen and uneven ground, and always like a tremendous surf beating on an iron shore comes the booming of the guns. Rockets shoot up, leaving a long green stream of stars, and showing up the silent country, snowbound, and very peaceful-looking, until one comes to a village totally deserted, ruined walls, heaps of débris, and great shell-holes in road and roof telling their dreadful story. And, as if a miracle had happened, there stands the church untouched. We halt silently, and move on again, and, as if to remind us that the world is not so peaceful after all, shells come bursting through the air. One bursts quite close, setting a ruined house in a tremendous blaze, and lighting up the whole scene (quite one for a painter).

" We are just out of it; five minutes earlier would have shown us all up, and we should probably have been very effectively shelled. We climb down little slippery slopes, and up others very warily (one is carrying everything, and the nails in one's boots on the hard ground make bad going). Over fields, and then we reach reserve trenches at about 7.30. I hate reserve trenches. One of my great fears is suffocation, and to stagger into a hole in the ground, and find oneself under the earth, head touching knees and roof above, in black darkness, not knowing where one is, and feeling caught in on every side is dreadful to me.

" We do guards, each section, till about 4.30 in the morning, with slight sniping to remind one of les Allemands, then we form up and off again, and stagger, it seems, for miles across fields and broken country. Here we are at last at the first line of trenches. Black, silent figures constantly appear, a few whispered orders, and we find ourselves in the trenches.

" There are five of us in our trench. The dawn comes slowly up and we can see what is in front of us. We are evidently on top of a slope or, rather, not quite on top. Snow-covered fields slope down to a ditch or small stream, overhung by clumps of willows ; a similar ditch runs up to our trenches on the left ; from the first ditch the ground slopes up again, and almost at the top one can see trenches (the enemy's) going right along, and the crest of the slope strongly outlined against the sky, with a shed or two and one or two chimneys showing up beyond it. There is to be one observer in every trench for half an hour all through the day, and at night an hour.

" The cold is still intense, but we open a tin of jam and start having breakfast. Suddenly my slice of bread and jam is covered with clay knocked off the top of the parapet. The snipers are at work, and wonderful shots they are too. Over a hundred bullets were put just in the top of our trench, and whenever an observer's head went up to look through a small enclosure they were at it again. Suddenly their batteries open fire on us, and, getting the range with marvellous celerity, they proceed in the next hour to put close on a hundred shells on about half a dozen trenches, including ours. We are all crouched down (our heads under our wings sort of business). The noise is appalling,

one's eardrums feel splitting as each shell bursts
and creeps nearer and nearer to our trench. Clouds
of black, evil-smelling smoke, showers of earth and
stones, mangel-wurzels, and pieces of shell, come
flying into the trenches. One man finds a large
piece of shell in his overcoat pocket. No one was
hurt of our lot. On our left the regiment had four
killed and several wounded. This is being under
fire properly, and we are glad they have stopped
and given us a rest. Not so the snipers, who keep
it up all day.

Night observation is very nerve-racking. Trees
move about, showing black against the snow, the
sky is very clouded, all shapes look human, menac-
ing and advancing. There is a tremendous artillery
duel going on on our left, like a million stage car-
penters knocking together a scene of herculean
proportions.

"Some Regulars come up to reinforce our
trench as an attack is expected. I can hear a tremendous movement of supply wagons going on
just over the hill-crest in the enemy's line. Some
red sparks show fitfully in the trenches, rockets
going up, and the sky is ever and anon split with
great flames of light. A farm behind our lines is
one great blaze, and they send up rocket signals
on our side back to headquarters, but nothing
happens.

"We are relieved just before dawn, and we
creep back here, very tired, dirty and cold, but very

glad to have got through our real first test of endurance all right."

" We are having the most damnable weather,
and for the last week we have been absolutely
drenched to the skin.   We have been several times
in the firing-line, but we have so far been awfully,
lucky, our casualties to date being about thirty
killed and wounded.

" I had far and away the biggest fright of my
life on November 25th or 26th; we were in the
firing-line trenches, and about 7 P.M. the order
came for a corporal and three men to go into a
listening or observation trench about a hundred
and fifty yards from our trenches and about two
hundred and fifty yards from the German trenches.
We waited and watched until about ten o'clock,
and then some Regulars on our right flank started
rapid fire, which was immediately taken up by
some more on our left.   It was awfully misty and
one could only see about thirty yards in front.

" We started back to our trench when one of
our section (who had misunderstood the order not
to fire until we four were back safe) started firing
in our direction.   The bullets were coming all
round our heads and into the belt of trees where we
were running, and I never thought for a moment
there was a chance of any of us getting back.   It
was simply wonderful how none of us got hit.   I
was nearly paralysed with funk, and then for an

hour we had a most exciting time; it was impossible, of course, in the darkness to see what numbers were against us, but the bullets came whistling past our faces in scores. They, luckily, were shooting too high, as they only killed three of us (only No. 1 Company was there that night).

" It was wonderful when one is fighting for one's life how fear absolutely disappears. We could see the flash from their rifles only about twenty-five yards away, and my one wish was that the devils would come right into our trenches so that we could have a good hand-to-hand fight. Our chaps did jolly well and kept up a very hot fire. I got off about a hundred and seventy rounds myself. Then the bullets began to get fewer, and after about an hour there was complete silence. We rather expected an attack, because they gave us an awful dose of ' Jack Johnsons ' in the morning; they were searching for our trenches for about an hour and a half, and gave us about fifty of those beastly coal-boxes, but they never, thank God, got the exact range.

" We had one frightfully cold night in the trenches, and our water in the water-bottles was frozen hard. Our brigade is now resting for a week, and we really deserve it as we have been working awfully hard.

" I had the most miserable time in my life two nights ago. We went into some reserve trenches which are 2 ft. wide and 2 ft. 6 in. deep. They are covered with straw and mud and sticks so as to be hidden; there is no room even to sit up, and they are absolutely dark. It began raining like blazes in the middle of the night, and went on incessantly; the water came pouring in, and, finally, after lying soaked to the skin in about three inches of mud and water, we had the order to evacuate them. It really was perfectly awful; we had nothing to change into as our bags, with a spare shirt and socks in, were full of mud and water.

" How I longed for a hot bath and some whisky and a nice warm bed! We were sent into an old bullet-ridden barn, and had three sows, some little pigs and a goat as bedfellows, but it was an absolute paradise to what we had just been experiencing.

" Last night we left at 7 o'clock, and got to bed at 1.30 this morning. It was raining the whole way and our kits seemed like lead; it is awfully heavy at the best of times, but when one's blanket and coat is soaked it is too awful to carry with a rifle and two hundred rounds of ammunition.

" I was fearfully exhausted when we got in this morning. We keep pretty cheerful really, although we are always grousing. I have got a charming lot of men in my section, and I know we are doing our bit. I should like to be in one terrific scrap in the day time before I come home, and none of us will be sorry when the war is over. Things are going very well, and we are going to get very good news soon."

The Mole's own correspondence at this time was limited to brief postcards.

Since leaving Le Mans the difficulties of getting a wash had increased greatly, and a bath was unheard of. As a makeshift the Mole was glad to get a change of underwear from home. Food now consisted almost entirely of bully beef, of which each man got a one-pound tin each day, hard biscuits much like dog-biscuits in appearance, with an occasional loaf of bread, and the much execrated plum and apple jam. This last was a yellowish viscous fluid not unlike machine oil to look at, and not much better to taste. Rumour had it that there *were* other more palatable varieties of jam, but either the sergeants' mess took charge or the A.S.C., sometimes known as the "jam-snatchers." Tea became a luxury, and mostly one's water-bottle was the only supply for quenching the thirst. Whenever opportunity offered the men would buy the flat circular loaves of Flemish bread, as the biscuits were very hard and trying for the teeth. All of this became better later on, and in rest billets the food was much as it had been at the advance base, while for the trenches tea was supplied to be brewed as required, though bully and biscuits were always the trench fare, unless eked out by private supplies.

Friday, November 27.—The battalion marched to Westoutre via Locre (soon to become very familiar). The billet was of the typical Flemish

farm type.   Most of the people about had at least
a smattering of French, though some spoke only
Flemish.   In such cases it was amusing and surprising to hear Highlanders carrying on some sort
of a conversation in broad Scotch, and how well
they got on with it.

The H.A.C. learned they were now part of the
7th Brigade, which included, in addition, the
famous Worcesters, the Wilts, the South Lancs
and the Royal Irish Rifles.   The 7th, 8th and 9th
Brigades constituted the 3rd Division, in the
Second Army Corps under Smith-Dorrien.

Regiments passing each other would inquire as
to their respective identities, thus :—

" Who are you? "

" We are the Honourable Artillery Company."

" Oh, are you?   Well, we are the *Honourable*
Middlesex ! "

Another conversation was reported as follows :

" So you are the H.A.C.   How many of you? "

" About 800."

" All volunteers aren't you? "

" Yes."

" —— fools ! "

Or, again, one Tommy calling to his pal :

" 'Ere, Bill, come and 'ave a look at a bloke
wot pide two guineas to come and fight ! "

Emergency rations were now issued.   Each
consisted of a pound tin of bully, about half a dozen
biscuits and the so-called " iron ration," a tin con-

taining a little tea and sugar, and a few cubes of Oxo. All of this was to be kept intact, and only to be used when ordered. It was inspected from time to time to see that it was so kept, as there was a great temptation towards the end of an exhausting march to throw away anything and everything to lighten the crushing load.

A very good impression of the general life is conveyed in an article entitled, " The Civilian in Battle," by Duncan Tovey, published in the *Weekly Dispatch:*

" The conditions of this war are so varied that two men of different battalions, or even of different companies in the same battalion, rarely get the same experience, and it is therefore hard to get a clear idea of what happened on any particular occasion from the accounts of individual soldiers. And as for getting an idea of what is going to happen, if you believe all that you hear you will be stuffed full ' on the very best authority told in confidence by a man who's in the know, who got it from the General Staff, or heard it up at G.H.Q.,' of a collection of facts sufficient to last you till the cows come home. ' Rumour, painted, full of tongues,' as the old play says, and full of tongues she certainly is. At the front nobody knows **anything,** but everybody has heard something, and each something is different from the last. Rumour gets busy when the battalion disembarks from the boat, and waits on the wharf while the fatigue parties unload the transport.

" Nobody knows when we are off, or where we are off to, but everyone has a theory, or has heard a rumour ' on the very best authority.' Then, probably one is bundled into a train, which, after the Continental manner in war-time, leaves leisurely for an unknown destination, probably having waited until nightfall to do so. One may spend any number of hours (generally exceeding twenty-four) in the aforesaid train, never knowing at what station one may get the order to get out. The train consists of horse-boxes, supposed to hold 36 to 40 men, but that is French measurement. Anything over 20 is like being in a pantomime pit crowd on a Saturday night, and the only way to get rid of your kit is to stand on it, or sit on the pack if there is room to sit at all. If it is warm enough to have the sliding doors open and sit with your feet outside, well and good, but on a cold winter day—' B-r-r ! Keep that —— door shut, can't yer? ' And the atmosphere becomes thicker than the very best extra special ' London particular.'

" So you get as comfortable as you can until a ruthless hand lets in the cold grey dawn on you and you are extracted, to shiver in the cold, cold world in a strange place, to face you know not what further discomforts, which you immediately begin to experience by trying to put on someone else's equipment by mistake, and getting purple in the face because the belt won't meet. And when after mutual recriminations you get your own it is hopelessly mixed up, the entrenching tool is entangled with the water-bottle, and in trying to get it straight the pouches come open, and all the ammunition drops in the mud.

" You speculate on the chances of getting any hot tea, but unless you are sure of a long wait and a statutory breakfast interval the chances are small. Probably the cooks have got all their stuff packed, and you have to fall back on what you may or may not have in your water-bottle. Perhaps billets are arranged for you in the neighbourhood, in which case you are marched off to them at once, and shown to your quarters, usually a barn or a loft over a cow-shed. There is generally plenty of straw and you manage to get a comfortable bed, and probably there will be either tea or stew from the cooks, and in any case coffee at 1d. per small bowl from the farm.

" So you settle down for the day or night, as the case may be. If you are allowed to take your boots off, so much the better. Usually you must be prepared to move at a moment's notice, and can't undo a bootlace or your pack. Oh, that pack! What a problem it becomes! Especially after the arrival of a mail. Three separate aunts or cousins send you a Balaclava helmet, you have a hundred cigarettes already of your favourite brand, and some misguided philanthropist sends you a large box of woodbines. You find yourselves landed with about half a hundredweight of 'comforts' and nowhere to put them. The end of it is that if you do have to move suddenly, half the things are left behind. If there is a good long march on the programme, nobody carries more than he can possibly help. It's wonderful what you can do without if you try. Who, in England, would think of wearing a shirt for a month or six weeks without taking it off, except for an occasional wash—not of the shirt, no such luck! The order to move off always comes when you are least expecting it, and probably have taken a chance and got your pack undone. You have most likely received a large parcel full of problems, and have not made up your mind what to take and what to throw away, and you set yourself to the task of trying to get a quart of luggage into a pint of pack, and are late on parade and get generally sworn at all round.

"Another problem is that of washing. When you get to the trenches or dug-outs, nobody ever thinks of such a thing. Water is generally very scarce, only to be obtained at considerable risk from snipers or shrapnel, generally from a farmhouse that has been destroyed, the pump perhaps surviving amid a mass of ruins. The water perhaps isn't as good as it might be, and orders are that it is not to be drunk unless boiled, but you are thirsty and have been inoculated against enteric, so you take a chance on it. Even when resting in billets a decent wash is hard to get. Probably there are a hundred or more of you on the farm, and only two buckets to be had, so if you get a lick and a promise it is all that can be hoped for as you struggle with a dull razor and cold water.

" And the mud! Never was there such mud since the Deluge dried up. You live in it, swim in it, splash in it all day long. Your boots are shapeless masses, and it is hopeless to keep them dry, let alone clean. If you walk along a road and meet any transport, you have to hop off the paved causeway in the middle into unknown depths at the side, and get generously splashed into the bargain. If you are lucky it's only a foot deep. But there may be a shell-hole disguised in it. On a long night march—most of the marches are at night—you sit down in it at the halts on your pack. It is a good dodge to sling it knapsack fashion on the supporting straps, so that you can take it off without undoing the rest of your equipment. And then the job of keeping the mud out of your rifle and ammunition! A very good dodge is to cut the stitches out of a spare bandolier and button it over the action. In the trenches, of course, mud is everywhere. If you lean up against the side it gets into your pouches and ammunition, and then your magazine jams and your rifle becomes useless.

" Going up to the trenches is an exciting

amusement. You move as noiselessly as possible along the side of the road (if there is one) in single file, and if you stumble into a shell-hole or over a wire you seem to make a terrible clatter. If the enemy are throwing light-bombs or star-shells, you get down and keep still while the light is on—one man moving may give you away and draw the enemy's fire—and then you go on again. Perhaps the enemy's trenches are only a hundred yards or so away, and you have to be careful, because it is in going up and back when you are in the open that men are likely to get hit. Sometimes you will be in a trench for a week with nothing happening except a few shells and an occasional sniper, but you never know your luck. That is the key-note of the whole business. You never know."

Monday, November 30.—The **H.A.C.** left Westoutre and were billeted near Scherpenberg, one of the few hills in the surrounding Flemish plain (between Locre and La Clytte). It must always be borne in mind that the various names only became known much later, as the men had no means of knowing their whereabouts. The pioneer section had been broken up for some little time, and the Mole was with his company, No. 4. The battalion had four companies, each nominally about 200 strong, and consisting of four platoons. Each platoon should thus have forty to fifty men under an officer, and comprising four sections under

N.C.O.'s. The greater part of the time was spent "standing by" waiting for orders or just plain waiting—waiting for food, waiting for the post, always waiting for the next thing, and never knowing what the next hour might bring.

Thursday, December 3.—The battalion was paraded on the road (Locre—La Clytte), and it was announced that the King would pass. The H.A.C. have a special cheer, known as "Artillery fire," and it was planned to shout this when the order was given. The men were in full equipment with pack, and were beginning to get tired of waiting for an hour or so, as per usual, when about three o'clock several motor cars passed rapidly by. It was hardly realised that the first contained the King, and it was almost past the line when the signal to cheer was given. In one of the following cars was the Prince of Wales, looking very young and startled. It is supposed that the King was taken to the top of Scherpenberg to get a view of Ypres and the surrounding country.

The battalion then formed up and marched off.

CHAPTER VIII

KEMMEL

THE men marched to Locre and then took a turn to the left on the road they were afterwards to know so well. Just as darkness was falling they breasted a steep slope where the road ran over the shoulder of a high hill (afterwards known to be Mont Kemmel) and as they passed a heavy shell burst near the top. As they observed later, on the top of the hill was a tower which the Germans evidently (though incorrectly) believed to be an observation post, for they shelled it systematically for several months before they obtained a hit, and even then only knocking part of the top off.

Then down the reverse slope and so on into a dark and deserted village, which by the light of the moon was seen to be much the worse for shell-fire. This, as the men found out later, was Kemmel, which for months was to be Brigade and Regimental Headquarters when the battalion was in the trenches. Kemmel is on the southern edge of the Wipers salient, opposite Wytschaete Ridge. Three companies disappeared, but No. 4 continued through the village and emerged beyond it. The order was given for single file, no talking and no lights or smoking. Evidently they were close to the firing line. The men crept along under the shadow of a hedge and eventually entered a trench.

This soon led to water, first ankle-deep, then up to the knee. Cursing their luck, the company floundered along after the officer leading the way. He also had enough of it, and, finally, all clambered out on to the top, only to find after all their stealthy precautions that a party of Chasseurs Alpines digging trenches near by were smoking cigarettes and chattering away unconcernedly. The night was bright but cold, and the men, very wet, were soon shivering. They were led to a ruined building and told they would spend the night there (presumably as reserves in case of emergency), but they must stand by for an instant move if called upon, and no equipment must be removed. Under these circumstances nothing could be done to mitigate their discomfort, and the men dozed off into uneasy and broken slumber.

By dawn they were up and away and led to so-called dug-outs (on the Kemmel—Kruisstraathoek road). Dug-outs, as they were known later, well constructed and well protected, did not exist in those days. These, for example, were simply formed by occupying a ditch by the side of the road, putting some twigs and branches across it and covering as might best be accomplished with straw, grass and, where available, odds and ends of boards in an attempt to gain some protection from the weather. How inadequate this was became evident only too soon. A steady downpour set in. Wet already, the men found, with disgust, that the rain soon penetrated their make-shift head-covering, and, in addition, the ditch was filling with water. Their condition got wetter and more miserable as the day went on. Then at night back to the ruins where they had spent the previous night, but this time avoiding the trench on the way there. Again the next morning to their dug-outs. Sodden with wet, the men gladly believed the rumour that by nightfall they would at least have the comparative comfort of farm billets. It was not to be. At dusk the company fell in and were told that they would relieve Regulars in the firing trench as they were exhausted. The company, already fatigued with exposure and little sleep, stumbled across wet fields to the rear of the trench, where they lay down waiting to relieve and listening to the hiss of bullets coming over. Gradually the outgoing soldiers trickled down the road one by one. They were the Royal Scots. Worn out with exposure, they staggered along, their teeth chattering as they went. Their coats, sopping with water and heavy with clay, flapped about their knees, and some seemed on the point of collapse, moaning piteously as they stumbled down the road.

The Company now made for the trench. Instead of moving up quietly as they should have done, they were ordered to make a dash for it. The consequent rattle and clatter must have given the Germans in the opposite trench the notion that an attack was taking place. They loosed off their

rifles and a machine-gun in rapid fire into the darkness, and it is marvellous that the Company was
not wiped out. Fortunately, owing to the darkness, casualties were wonderfully few. On reaching
the trench it was found that one part simply could
not be occupied, it was so bad. One man promptly
got bogged to the waist, and it was several hours
before a party could extricate him. Even in the
parts of the trench that could be and were occupied
conditions were very bad, nothing but semi-liquid
mud, and stepping off a sandbag or a stray bit of
board meant plunging into it from ankle depth to
over the knee. The men huddled themselves
together, making what they could in the way of
cutting some sort of place to sit, but little could be
achieved. Day broke after a night that seemed
endless, and they found themselves opposite a wood
(Petit Bois). As soon as daylight came everyone
was busy attempting to clean his rifle, all of them
being jammed with clay in spite of the protective
swathings. Eventually the day also passed, and
at last they were relieved.

Those three days, followed by the ensuing
march to billets, broke the back of No. 4 Company.
The cold and wet knocked out a lot of the men.
The exposure had the effect of thoroughly exhausting everybody, and the march back to billets was
a terrible ordeal. Half the men of No. 4 never got
there that night at all, straggling by the wayside.
It must be remembered that in addition to the

weight usually carried, a thoroughly wet overcoat, thickly plastered with clay, is appallingly heavy. In fact, it can hardly be lifted with one hand. The destination was Westoutre, but on arriving there after an awful tramp the remnant nearly mutinied when they found they had another two miles to go beyond the village. Even the Mole found his endurance taxed to the utmost limit and only just managed to stagger in. Another hundred yards would have been too much. Many of the men did not even manage to get their boots off before falling into a stupor of complete exhaustion.

Although trenches gradually improved as time went on, this is an example of what they were like in the early days of the Wipers Salient. The terrible march back to billets was commemorated in the alphabet:

" X is the extra two miles that we do
When we get to Westoutre and have to go
        through."

It seemed to rain continually and never a chance to get really dry.

French writes in his dispatch dated February 2nd, 1915: " The troops composing the Army in France have been subjected to as severe a trial as it is possible to impose upon any body of men. Frost and snow have alternated with periods of continuous rain. The men have been called upon to stand for many hours together almost up to their waists in bitterly cold water, only separated by one or two hundred yards from a most vigilant enemy."

There were no Y.M.C.A. huts where men could dry themselves, and only later were gumboots served out to troops entering the trenches. The toll taken by exposure was high. Frostbitten feet, or, more correctly, "trench feet," disabled large numbers. British troops coming from India lost nearly half their numbers in a short space of weeks through exposure alone.

The H.A.C. now took their turn regularly with their brigade when it went to the trenches, Kemmel being the forward headquarters, and either Westoutre or mostly Locre being the rest billets. When in the trenches they occupied the F sector of trenches opposite Wytschaete Ridge. Conditions were made more bearable by steady work on improving the trenches, taking up boards to stand on, etc.

Each man going up would also take his little supply of wood, so as to be able to brew tea over a "fire-bucket." In these early days the trenches particularly in the clay of "The Salient" were nothing but undrained ditches. Clips of S.A.A. (Small Arms Ammunition) dropped were immediately engulfed in the mud. In fact, whole boxes of S.A.A. used to stand on gradually disappeared, and eventually were entirely buried several feet deep. Thousands and thousands of rounds must have been lost in this way.

[LETTER]

"December 20, 1914.

" For the first time in weeks I now have an opportunity of getting another letter written. Cigarettes have become fairly plentiful now.   I do not see any likelihood of leave.

" With regard to the commission, I believe the declination to make a recommendation was due to a question of policy, as there are so many qualified men in the battalion that there would be few left if all took commissions. For the moment we are, as an exception, resting without orders to be ' standing by,' which means ready to move off at a moment's notice. A large amount of time is spent like this, with all equipment on, and it prevents one doing anything.

" Though we have been under shell-fire from time to time, the trenches are pretty well protected. All movement, marching, getting to and from trenches, etc., is done at night, and means stumbling over awful roads, pitted with shell-holes, and across a morass of fields. If the Germans send up a star-shell at that time, one has to duck down and remain motionless until the light of it goes out.   The greatest danger is really from ' snipers ' who conceal themselves in hay-ricks, etc., by day inside our lines, and pot at you as soon as it gets dusk. On the other hand, firing from the enemy's trenches is quite haphazard at night, as they cannot see anything. The trenches, though fairly safe, are devilish uncomfortable, and I have sat for hours with water over the tops of my boots.

" I have not been replying to individual letters as opportunities are scarce, and one is so frequently dead-beat that you simply flop down to sleep whenever you get the chance.

" The eatables have all been welcome, as our diet has been practically confined to cold 'bully.' Hot tea, when we can get it, is a godsend. We have been having a pretty strenuous time all round, and are badly in need of a real rest."

[LETTER]
"*December* 21, 1914.

" For some time past we have been hard at it, either in the firing-trenches, or as supports and reserves. The weather and general conditions have been very trying—almost continuous rain. The roads and trenches are consequently very bad. At the best the trench is wet and muddy, and in the worst places some of the men have been bogged to the waist for hours before they could be extricated. We usually go up for three days, either in the firing-trenches or supports, and then three days as reserves, billeted in a neighbouring village or barns. One's feet are perpetually sodden with water, and frequently one is pretty wet besides; and with no chance to get dry it is really remarkable, after sleeping as best we may in the trench, why we don't all get crocked up. We take turn about at half-hour guards to watch for attacks. After straining your eyes in the dark for some time you can imagine almost anything in front of you.

" I keep quite well on the whole, though a prolonged diet of cold ' bully ' and biscuits has made me subject to indigestion. Still, the life, and a certain amount of mental strain, take it out of you tremendously, and you feel that you have no reserve of strength to draw on. Even the short marches of a few miles between trenches and billets are quite exhausting.

" Once in the trench there is comparatively little danger, as you are well protected. It is on the way to and from it that there is some risk of being ' sniped.'

" I haven't had a bath for ages, and frequently have to go for a week without even a wash or shave. We hope to get a little rest one of these days."

CHAPTER IX

CHRISTMAS, 1914

CHRISTMAS was uneventful, except in so far as it was spent in the trenches, by now somewhat improved in their condition. Reports reached the H.A.C. that fraternising had taken place with the enemy in some parts of the line (believed to have been the case at " Plugstreet "), but nothing of that kind was evident in their sector. The day was celebrated by the distribution of the " Princess Mary boxes," a neat little brass box containing a pipe and smoking materials, to all the troops at the Front.

By this time the original eight hundred had been reduced to about half their strength, partly by casualties, mostly incurred on the way to or from the trenches, but even more so by the results of exposure, trench feet, rheumatism, etc., necessitating invaliding home.

Locre had now become the usual place for the rest interval, the main billets being in an uncompleted school building (uncompleted as to partitions, etc.) adjoining a convent. The Mole and some friends got permission to billet themselves in the vestry of the church, just across the way. The sisters were pleased to be of assistance to the men, and made them free of their kitchen for hot water, etc. One of the sisters turned out to be Irish, having come from an Irish convent at Ypres.

Whenever the brigade was in rest billets the various battalions took it in turn to supply the men required for fatigue parties, etc. One battalion was always detailed to be ready to move off to the firing-line absolutely complete at fifteen minutes' notice, at any hour of the day or night. One time, when it came to be the turn of the H.A.C., there were circumstantial rumours that a test turn-out would be ordered and the time required would be carefully noted and compared with that of other records. So everybody lay down, practically ready to jump to his feet on the signal. Sure enough about midnight one of the billet guards on sentry duty saw a figure appear in the darkness and heard the order " Turn out." Each guard stuck his head in the doorway and bawled out the same order. With a clatter of arms and equipment the battalion burst out into the street. The N.C.O.'s paraded the men and checked over their sections, ready to report " All present " in record time as soon as the officers appeared. Nothing happened. Finally a messenger was sent over to the orderly room. It was dark and deserted. Eventually the whole thing turned out to be a hoax, and the perpetrator was never discovered. The various sentries were all keyed up for the expected order and no one had thought of questioning the man who first shouted it.

All the main activities took place during the hours of darkness, as the enemy could overlook and observe much of our ground from his ridges. The march from rest billets was always timed to reach Kemmel Hill after dark, and those for duty in the trenches would continue up to them, slithering and sliding over greasy clay fields in single file. On dark nights one could hardly see the man in front, and it was difficult not to lose touch. Burdened with extra loads, a man would have difficulty in crossing even the smallest ditches or any other obstacles, and nearly everybody would fall into some hole or other on the way up. Every check made itself felt all the way to the rear, and no matter how slowly those in front moved forward those behind had frequently to run to catch up. Orders passed down by word of mouth were frequently strangely distorted so as to be quite unintelligible.

On arriving in the trench the men would take the places of the regiment to be relieved, fix bayonets and see that rifles were in working order, a necessary precaution, as, owing to falling down, etc., the action was nearly always jammed with clay, in spite of attempts at protection. Every fourth man or so would be detailed for sentry duty, while the others busied themselves with the various activities of the night, filling sandbags, repairing breaches in the trench, ration parties, etc. Dusk and dawn were the most likely hours for an attack by the enemy, and for an hour before each " stand to " (stand to arms) was ordered, each man at his place and ready. Slowly the night passes, and finally the long-drawn-out desolation of dawn reveals the gleaming watery waste. After " stand to " only a few sentries are required to keep a look-out with a periscope, the remainder eat their breakfast and are free to achieve what rest and comfort they can, huddling on the fire-step like homeless dogs. Dug-outs did not exist, and the most protection that could be had was by rigging up something with a " wetter-sheet," which always gave way when most needed.

Shelling by the enemy was not heavy as compared with later days. Our own guns were still less active. They were few in number; it was said that each gun was limited to " one round per gun per day perhaps! " When the enemy did bombard our trenches our guns often did not reply at all, making one feel furious and helpless at the preponderance of the enemy artillery. It is a sickening thing to have to endure shelling without being able to reply to it in any way. From time to time " artillery duels " were reported in the Press. Actually this meant that the artillery was shelling the trenches of the other side, and it was the P.B.I. who got it in the neck. Batteries, designed to fire with open sights, had now perforce to use indirect fire from protected positions where they remained undisturbed for weeks on end. To those in the trenches the gunners' life seemed like a haven of rest. This also changed in the later course of the war when the gunners suffered heavy casualties from counter-battery work.

Letter from the trenches by another member of the H.A.C. (*Evening News*) :—

" The French have only recently taken this position from the Germans and to our right are numerous dead bodies lying about in contorted attitudes. The enemy is only about eighty yards away, and, consequently, neither side exposes itself overmuch. Next to us is our Maxim-gun, and there is a gap between our trenches so that we have to keep a careful look-out, especially by night."

From *The Times* :—" A member of the H.A.C. writes :

" ' The trenches are awful—in places three or four feet deep in water—and frostbite is pretty general. I am still fit, but rheumatic.

" ' On Thursday last a shell came into the trench and burst right in the middle of our section, but not one of us was touched. The same day Corporal ——, an old golfing friend of mine, was shot dead through a loop-hole. Such is fate ! Also on the same day an enterprising German crept up to —— trench with a hand grenade. The fuse was bad, and it blew his hand off, and two of our men took him prisoner.

" ' We are brigaded with three well-known Regular regiments, and now do exactly the same work and go through the same routine as they do. I think we are earning a very good name for solid, non-theatrical work, but we are losing some jolly good men. Imagine an unceasing drizzle of fine

rain, acres of ploughed fields with an average of
12 in. of mud, scores of dead bodies rising to the
surface, an indescribable stench from these, and
acres of rotten turnips, ruined farms and villages,
not a light shown anywhere, an indescribable
atmosphere of dreariness and misery, a terrific
bombardment, shells everywhere, and yet not a
single battery or soldier, German or English, to be
seen anywhere—all under cover.

" ' Standing out in relief is the glorious British
Tommy with his superb courage, good humour and
courtesy.   I saw one of the Tommies we relieved
a little while ago fall down when coming out of the
trenches from fatigue and frozen feet.   He crawled
up and asked us to hold his hands so that he might
feel some warmth, and then, remembering that we
were just going into the same trench, hastened to
reassure us by saying he was all right, ' only a bit
numb.' "

CHAPTER X

1915

[LETTER]

" January 2, 1915.

" THE ' Artists ' is, of course, specifically an O.T.C. regiment, but we see many young lads as officers out here. What I said about commissions was never told me officially—I simply have that impression.

" I have sufficient money, but one cannot buy anything up here. The twice weekly idea for parcels is a good one. I had thought of it before, but did not want to make too much trouble. We are always changing quarters, and everything has to be carried in one's pack. Since wearing out my own boots I have been wearing Army boots, which are quite good, though no boots that I know of will keep your feet dry in the deep slush we have had to contend with. The weather is very wet again.

" You have no doubt seen various H.A.C. letters in *The Times*, which are substantially correct, and will inform you about details I have not mentioned.

" The ' Tommies ' really are splendid, and the way they have stuck it is marvellous.

" The pioneers are now to take on a new job. Since reaching the zone of active operations they had little special work to do, and have been going into the firing-line like anybody else.   They are now to work under the R.E., trying to improve the state of the trenches.   In fact, they will be, I gather, a sort of R.E. corps attached to their own battalion and working for them.

" My previous letters have told you about the trenches, and there is nothing I can think of to add.   My indigestion is better, but I have had touches of rheumatism, though I am glad to say I have escaped frost-bitten feet.   On the whole I get along quite well, and I hope you won't worry too much about me."

The pioneers now came into their own.   It had been announced that the pioneer section was to be reconstituted and increased from ten in number to twenty-five, each battalion in the brigade doing the same.   This body of men was commanded by the brigade pioneer officer, who, as a matter of fact, was a lieutenant of the H.A.C.

[LETTER]

" *January* 9, 1915.

" We had no truce on our part of the line at Christmas, though there was not much firing.   It was not bad, as everybody had loaded up with extra parcels of eatables for the occasion, and the weather for a day was passably fine.   I am afraid regular boots are the only practicable thing on account of marching.

" I am always much interested in any news you send, business or otherwise. The cutting from the *Westminster* re sappers was quite timely, as the pioneers have been calling themselves by that name. The work has been interesting, though fairly strenuous. Making barbed wire entanglements, fascines (Anglicé faggots 4 to 9 ft. in length), very useful for making a bottom to the water-logged trenches, carrying up sand-bags by hundreds, etc. The pioneers make these things during the day as well as carry them up to the trenches every night; but, on the other hand, get a comparatively decent sleep when they do get back late in the night or early morning hours. Some of the trenches are now provided with steel loophole plates, and in others, where the water is particularly bad, tubs are provided with the idea of men sitting in them, and thus avoid being in the water all the time. Anything in this direction is all to the good, though even in the best trenches sitting in the rain is not too amusing, particularly as one is bound to get very wet crossing sopping fields getting to them.

" I am feeling fairly fit, and getting along all right."

It was always a great relief to start back to Locre after a spell, and as soon as Kemmel Hill was passed men would light up and start a marching song, if not too tired. The favourite, to the

tune of " Hold your hand out, naughty boy!' "
was :—

   " Keep your head down, H.A.C.;
     Keep your head down, H.A.C.,
     Or a ruddy great hun, with a ruddy big gun,
     Will shoot yer, will shoo-oot yer!
     If you want to get back to the City Road,
     Keep your head down, H.A.C."

This was varied with " Oh, I don't want to die;
I want to go home! "

The H.A.C. were always a considerable puzzle
to the Regulars with whom they were brigaded,
and were always being mistaken for officers, particularly at night when only the voice could be
heard. The Mole had now acquired a Burberry
in place of the regulation coat which he dumped
at the convent at Locre (presumably it is there
yet), and in this he had the amusing though em-
barassing experience of walking the length of the
village holding a large lump of raw meat in his
hand, and receiving salutes from all sides, salutes
which he neither dared nor wished to " take."

One of the Worcesters wrote home (after an
impromptu concert by the H.A.C. at Locre):

" We have the H.A.C. ' Terriers ' in our
brigade and they are ' toffs.' They feel proud to
fight with the Worcesters and they are doing very
good work with a good heart. It seems hard to

see gentlemen like them roughing it. Our chaps admire them.

" Some of them are lords' sons, and you ought to hear them talk. They gave a concert the other night and it was splendid—just like professionals."

There was a good deal of bitterness at the difficulty of getting a commission, especially as all knew that at home they were being handed out indiscriminately.

[LETTER]

" *January* 17, 1915.

" Parcels and papers arriving all right. Christmas Day was not marked by any special features, except that we saved a few eatables, such as plum pudding, to take with us for the occasion. The long menu in the letter in the paper really means very little if you look into it a bit, and, in any event, looks rather faked. Oil for boots is not necessary; I get hold of grease from time to time; dubbin would be quite good.

" I am feeling comparatively fit now, a good deal better than I did. You are quite correct about the nature of the work, which is quite interesting in its way. I believe our efforts are quite appreciated by the authorities. I know quite definitely that commissions are only to be had on the recommendation of the C.O., and unless he sees fit to give it, there is nothing doing. I also happen to know that efforts to get around this are inadvisable, as one man I know of incurred a reprimand.

" Some new underwear will be acceptable soon, but before sending please sprinkle well with paraffin and then let it dry. Through sleeping in dirty barns, etc., many of the men have been troubled with vermin, and this is recommended as a preventive. I have so far been free, thank goodness !

" It is no good thinking about arranging a meeting. There is so little that I can tell you that I cannot give much in the way of news. Our men now do a turn of four days in the trenches, half of the men doing two spells of twenty-four hours, alternating with the other half, then four days' relief. A large draft has arrived, bringing us well up to strength again. The trenches are much the same.

" The postal service seems to be wonderfully well organised, as very little goes astray."

Bairnsfather has been criticised for depicting an " unsoldierly type " in his famous drawings. They were very true to life. Men muffled themselves in all sorts of weird wrappings in the endeavour to protect themselves from the inclement weather—mufflers round their heads, sacking over their shoulders or even as super-puttees. One man was adorned with a large piece of linoleum, the checkerboard pattern of which on his back was visible from

afar. " Old Bill " could be found over and over
again amongst the Regulars.

[LETTER]
" January 24, 1915.

" We have had numerous rumours of relief, but
that is as far as it goes, rumour being one of the
most plentiful things in the Army. My own particular guess is that the bulk of reinforcements will
be kept back until the weather is more favourable.

" Yes, the work suits me better, and though
the weather continues very sloppy I'm feeling
comparatively fit.

"Sometimes on the way to the trenches star
shell after star shell goes up from the German lines.
I suppose they are panicky and fear an attack. As
a matter of fact, the light, though apparently brilliant, does not show things up very distinctly, and
I do not believe they can see any distance beyond
their own trenches. I believe most of the casualties in the present stage of trench warfare are sheer
flukes, except for systematic shelling, which the
Germans do not seem to be doing. I think the
snipers are being gradually rounded up."

[LETTER]
" January 25, 1915.

" Things go on much as usual. We go up to
' close billets ' when our time for the trenches is
due. Those men not actually in the trenches stay

in a semi-ruined and semi-inhabited village near by,
which is shelled from time to time without much
damage being done.   When relieved we march to
a village a few miles back of the firing-line and billet
there.   We have lived in all kinds of places—barns,
pig-styes, schools, any unoccupied building, and
even a church; in fact, anywhere with a roof or
portion of one to cover our heads.   We are kept
quite busy all the time or else ' standing by ' ready
to move.   I am called off to work now."

French writes in his dispatch of February 2nd,
1915 :—

" In my dispatch of November 20th, 1914, I
referred to the reinforcements of Territorial troops
which I had received and I mentioned several units
which had already been employed in the fighting
line. . . . I and the principal commanders serving
under me consider that the Territorial Force has
far more than justified the most sanguine hopes
that any of us ventured to entertain of their value
and use in the field.

" Army corps commanders are loud in their
praise of the Territorial battalions which form part
of nearly all the brigades at the front in the first
line, and more than one of them has told me that
these battalions are fast approaching—if they have
not already reached—the standard of efficiency of
Regular infantry."

[LETTER]

February 2, 1915.

" I have been using grease and oil on my feet, but question whether of much virtue. If anything, it seems to feel colder, though it may be of value as preventing actual frostbite. Since organised work on the trenches has started much has been done to improve and strengthen the defences in our efforts to make it comfortable for our men and uncomfortable for the Germans. This last refers particularly to barbed wire entanglements made of a specially constructed trestle arrangement so that they can be taken up to the trenches and set out from there. Many of these have been constructed, to say nothing of hurdles, fascines, stakes and planks, all of which are most useful for improving the trench. In some cases overhead protection is now available. Our early experiences of the trenches saw them at their worst, though even now, after a spell of rain, they are pretty bad in places, and ploughing across the sodden fields means getting pretty wet. A list has been taken of public schoolmen in the battalion, and I have put my name in. I do not know whether it means anything in the way of commissions.

" In spite of our various trials and tribulations, we have managed to get a good deal of fun out of things, and I have spent some quite jolly evenings in billets.

" Have you heard the following? Tommy,

arrested for assaulting a French sentry, recounts how it happened : ' Halte là. Qui vive,' sez 'e. ' Je,' sez I, knowing the language. ' Où est votre lanterne? ' ' Elle est sortie ' ' Comment? ' sez 'e. ' Come on yourself,' sez I, and then the fight was on.

" I have not struck any of the luxurious baths that one reads about in the papers, but managed to get quite a decent tub bath in a cottage the other day. It was quite an event. Even washing can only be accomplished with considerable difficulty.

" Now that the Kaiser's birthday is safely passed, I suppose there is no harm in saying that we rather looked for a heavy attack and were ready to turn out at any hour of the night or day in case supports were required. We were not in the trenches at that time. I don't know how other parts of the line fared, but with us the day was not marked by any special effort on the part of the Germans. I just see they were active elsewhere."

[LETTER]

" *February* 10, 1915.

" Most of our writing (to say nothing of living, eating, etc.) is done squatting on the ground, chairs and tables, of course, usually being conspicuously absent, though a stray box is eagerly seized upon.

" The paraffined underwear is not an un-qualified success, as it is rather itchy and irritating to the skin, so that I had to apply vaseline to counteract the paraffin.

"Some of our men (O.T.C., I believe) have been getting commissions—just a few from each company. In such cases the man goes to the advance base, where he receives a course of instruction for several weeks. He is then assigned to one of the regiments out here and joins them. Uniform, etc., is of little importance, and he may go up again in the ordinary tunic with just a star added to the shoulder-strap. There has been a good deal of discussion as to the advantages and drawbacks of taking a commission. In the first place, a man has apparently no choice of regiment. Besides that, whatever happens to the battalion (possibly returning to England at some future date) he would continue for the remainder of the war. Finally, there is the question of greater risk, as officers seemed to be picked off. Some people call it the Suicide Club. Personally, of course, I should be only too pleased to get a chance at it.

"Some of the fragments of shells are thrown a terrific distance. A shell bursting on the road threw a piece of its base fully 500 yards away. Incidentally we repaired the shell-hole."

[LETTER]

"*February* 12, 1915.

"I saw V. this morning for a few minutes. His regiment is expected to go into the trenches

a few miles away from our own position. **He**
spoke of seeing you in Town.

"I have again put my name in for a commission; R.E. preferred, but willing to go into a line
regiment. I do not know whether anything will
come of it.

"The Germans took to potting at one of the
roads we used, so we turned out the other night
to chop down trees in a near-by wood, replanting
them alongside the road to act as a screen, so that
the Germans could not see when transport was on
the way. Some of their shells had torn huge holes.
The rain is less continuous than previously, though
the ground has little chance to dry out. Still, an
occasional glimpse of the sun is quite cheery.

"We have now had such large drafts out that
I hear the Second Battalion is nearly wiped out.
Our casualties have been comparatively small, but
a good many men have been invalided for one
reason or another."

[LETTER FROM THE HON. A. G. C. V. TO H. G.]
"*Oxfordshire Yeomanry,*

"*February* 11, 1915.

"My DEAR G.,—A curious chance brought me
to where W. is billeted at Locre; he was building
hutments—looking the picture of health and smoking a priceless cigar, and in great spirits. I don't
think he has got fatter like B. says I have, but he
looked as well as ever.

" I went to Ypres to-day on a joy-ride ; there were quite a number of shells dropping about. It felt quite strange having been out of it for so long. The Cloth Hall and church have got a real knocking about, but there are still quite a number of shops open.

" I do hope that W. will keep fit. I admired him enormously for joining as a private. He knew what he was in for, and he got it. But he was as cheery as possible when I saw him, and that is more than half the battle."

[LETTER]

" *February* 18, 1915.

" I quite understand that tinned stuff should not be left in the tin after opening, but am satisfied that there is practically no danger. Probably the various kinds of dirt that may accompany the meal is a more likely source of trouble. I note wader stockings, and will see how they turn out. The difficulty with all these things is that they are extra weights, and also if really waterproof retain all the perspiration.

" We continue our work as usual, but there are rumours of impending changes. According to these the battalion is to furnish some men for commissions (which leads me to hope), others for sniping work, and still others for various specialised jobs for which they are fitted, while the sappers are to continue but work for the division as a

,whole.   Rumours are unusually unreliable, but nous verrons! We understand the authorities are well pleased with the work of the battalion, including sappers.''

[LETTER]

" *February* 21, 1915.

" At the present moment all new rumoured arrangements for the battalion are knocked on the head by a transfer to another section of the Army, though we remain in the same district. I do not know what effect this will have on applications for commissions. People at home seem to get them with great ease.

" The Germans have shown much greater activity up here of late, apparently also on other parts of the line.

" We have continued our usual work, but the recent transfer may mean upsetting the existing arrangement, though I hope not. The whole thing may be temporary. The weather is rather trying again.

" I had the opportunity to watch the firing of a 6-in. gun. This does not sound very big, but it really is a pretty big affair. When fired it fairly rears in the air like a restive horse, though the report is not as loud as one might anticipate. There are, I believe, much bigger guns out here, and still bigger to come.''

[LETTER]

"*February* 27, 1915.

" The underwear is all right now. We might try less sprinkling when the next lot is sent out.

" Yes, I know R., and am glad you saw him. He was quite correct as to numbers (*only about 300 of the original H.A.C. left*). Rest rumours are ever rife and always being disproved. Yes, I thought of ' Birnam Wood ' at the time (referring to camouflaging the road).

" I have often considered a flash lamp, but decided against the extra weight. Much snow of late—very slushy. Our usual work continues, I am glad to say. We have been supplying enormous quantities of material, sand-bags, etc., to the trenches.

" We hear rumours of 15-in. guns and 21-in. howitzers to come up to this district! I have seen preparations for some heavy foundation, or I would otherwise discredit it altogether; it sounds so tremendous.

" My ' panic postcard ' was sent off the same day as the letter, in case the latter was delayed at all. The p.p.cs can be handed in without formalities, whereas a letter means much red tape.

" Our people captured a German (Bavarian) in rather a curious way the other day. He was sent out to ascertain if one of our trenches was occupied, and was returning to his own lines when the Germans opened fire on him. In an effort to detour he lost his way, and finally landed in another section of our trenches. They are apparently still full of confidence."

[LETTER]

"*March* 8, 1915.

" Work continues much as usual.

" We notice the Germans seem to be very panicky just now. Star-shell follows star-shell at night, accompanied by a volleying fire, which is presumably intended to ward off a feared attack. No doubt you realise that all letters are still being censored, and that I sometimes hear news which it is not advisable to communicate. This limits the scope of a letter."

This last paragraph referred to an impending attack, which is reported by French as follows :—

" The General Officer Commanding the Second Corps arranged for an attack on a part of the enemy's position to the south-west of the village of Wytschaete which he had timed to commence at 10 A.M. on March 12th. Owing to dense fog the assault could not be made until 4 o'clock in the afternoon.

" It was then commenced by the Wiltshires and Worcestershire Regiments, but was so hampered by the mist and the approach of darkness that nothing more was effected than holding the enemy to his ground."

For several days before there was great activity through the brigade. Trench ladders were constructed and taken up, etc. On the day itself there was great suspense as to the cause of the delay. As noted above, it was on account of the mist, which prevented observers for the artillery from making the required observations. Finally the attack was launched only to be beaten back by heavy machine-gun fire. The gallant Worcesters and Wilts made a desperate effort to reach their objective, but their casualties were heavy and the attack failed.

CHAPTER XI

IN THE SAPPERS

As will have been seen from the preceding letters, the Mole had put in his name for a commission again, and this time with better luck as far as the preliminary steps were concerned.   After giving particulars of education, branch of service desired, etc., Taffy finally allowed it with some others to go to Brigade headquarters.   One day the Brigadier turned up, and some twenty applicants were paraded for his inspection.   He stated that he had come to see them as he had to say that he had actually done so before he could approve their applications and pass them on.   He added the usual exhortations, and wound up by saying : " And if you become officers don't hide round a corner when you see me coming, not knowing whether to salute or not as so many young fellows do, but salute smartly and show you're not scared."

The Mole felt that the much sought after commission was at last coming his way, but before it actually resulted from this inspection another interview took place.

On March 9th the H.A.C. were in their usual rest billets in Locre when word was passed round that the C.O. wanted all men with mining experience to report to him.   A number, including the Mole, did so.   After questioning the various men and weeding out most of them, only three being left, the C.O. said there was a chance to get into mining—" a risky business, but with good prospect of kudos." The Mole and his companions said they were willing to take the chance.

Then they were interviewed by a Lieutenant-colonel in the Sappers who cross-examined them as to their experience and knowledge, and, finally, as Taffy interposed " They have all three been recommended for a commission," he took their names and said he would forward them to G.H.Q. for approval.

The battalion then moved off to Kemmel.

On March 13th the Mole was in the woods near by directing a party of Brigade pioneers from the other battalions in the making of fascines when he was ordered to report to the C.O. " at once." Dirty with the work and wearing mud-splashed gumboots, he clumped into the temporary orderly room not knowing just what was coming, but hoping for the best. His hopes were realised.

Taffy greeted him, " Good afternoon, *Mister* G.," which told the tale at once. He continued, " I congratulate you on being posted to the Royal Engineers. The adjutant will give you your train order."

" The R.T.O., Bailleul.

The undermentioned men of the H.A.C. have been ordered to report themselves to the Chief

Engineer, G.H.Q., they having been appointed to temporary commissions in the R.E. : —

  Pte. W. G——
   ,, H. W——
   ,, H. D. M——
     (Signed) T. L. Walsh,
13/3/15.   Capt. and Adjt. H.A.C."

There was jubilation in the pioneer billet that night, all heartily congratulating the Mole. The O.C. section came round and added his good wishes, very kindly giving a couple of his bronze stars so that the Mole could at once put them on the shoulder straps of his tunic. Rather a curious incident occurred. The Mole knocked over a candle (rather a thicker one than usual), it fell, landed upright, and continued burning. The others at once hailed it as a good omen.

[LETTER]

" March 13, 1915.

" You will be interested to hear that I have obtained a commission in the R.E. This is the result of an application I put in some little time ago. It is for mining work. I am to report to G.H.Q. (out here) and will then know more about the future. The chances are I shall go to work at once."

The Mole found his two companions, who had been similarly informed, and they proceeded to

Locre, where they spent the night. There was considerable discussion as to whether they would get any leave. On the next day they got a lift in the mess-cart ("Gorringe") to Bailleul and boarded the afternoon train to St. Omer, arriving there late at night.

They reported to the office of the Chief Engineer where, after a long wait, they saw Major N. G., who gave them a long talk, and, finally, to their delight, made out leave papers, telling them exactly what train to catch for the return. They slept the night at an hotel—in bed for the first time for months.

Up early next morning, they boarded the leave train, the Mole sending the following telegram :—

"March 15, 1915.

" Have obtained commission. Returning home four days' leave. Arrive this evening."

The Mole arrived home that night. He had three clear days before returning. There was a great bustle to get uniform and outfit. To the credit of the enterprising firm of Burberry's, be it said, that he walked in there at 9.30 in the morning, and by the same evening dined in complete kit.

On March 19th the Mole met his two companions at the station to catch the 6 o'clock train, as directed. At first, to their consternation, they learned that the time of the train had been changed to an earlier hour and it had already left. Then,

as they realised they had a valid excuse for practically an extra day, their feelings changed to
delight. Finally, they got away on the 20th,
landed at Boulogne, and proceeded to St. Omer,
and thence to Bailleul.

[LETTER]

" *March* 23, 1915.

" We had an uneventful crossing, moderately
rough, but not sufficiently so to disturb me at all.
After landing we found out that the train would
not be in till late, so we had dinner in the town
before driving down to the goods station where the
supply train, by which we were to travel, started
from.   A first-class carriage was attached, so we
had a comfortable trip.   We left about midnight,
arriving at G.H.Q. early next morning, where we
had a few hours' more sleep in another railway
carriage.   We then reported ourselves in.   No
questions asked as to the 6 o'clock train!   Major
N. G. was not there this time.   We left there that
evening, arriving here (B——) Sunday night.
Certainly travelling as an officer is considerably
more comfortable, as you can get people to help
you.

" At present things are rather confused as the
whole business is quite new.   Some work is already
going on, and within the next day or two we should
be also starting.   We are under Captain Johnson,
V.C.   He got the V.C. for his work on the Aisne,

ferrying a pontoon under fire, I believe. We have been helping him a little with organising things.

" J. is the C.O. of the 172nd Company, which is divided into four sections, each supposed to have two subalterns. As a motor lorry is attached, there should be no difficulty about carrying all our stuff except when we are actually in the trenches, which will probably be for two days on and two days off. All this part of it is rather hazy as yet, and we shall know more about it later on. Taking it on the whole, it looks like very strenuous times when at work, but quite a decent time when resting.

" When things are more settled we shall be organising a little mess for those not at work. We have seen some of our old regiment at L——, but hear they expect to be moving rather further along the line.

" The weather is much better now and I hope it will continue so."

The three names had appeared in G.H.Q. orders, but the actual gazetting was not published until later when they were already back and supervising operations.

The *London Gazette* Supplement, April 1, 1915 :—

REGULAR FORCES.

The following promotions to be made for service in the field :—

CORPS OF ROYAL ENGINEERS

To be temporary second lieutenants : Pte. W. G——, Pte. H. W——, Pte. H. D. M——, all from H.A.C. (March 9).

The following from the " Engineering and Mining Journal " (New York), June 12th, 1915, shows how history is made :—

" The British appear to be wasting a large percentage of their best human material in their process of ' muddling along ' in the war, but occasionally their eyes are opened. There are many in this country who know W. G., son of H. G., managing director of H. R. M. & Co. Young G. studied mining engineering at Columbia. Soon after the outbreak of the war he enlisted in the British Army, and went to the Front. It is told of him that after serving as a private in the trenches for about six months some sapping plans were inaugurated at the point where he was. Therein his mining experience played a useful part, of course, and attracted the attention of his superiors, who obtained the idea that such knowledge could be employed better than in the ranks. Consequently young G. was sent home for a little training in military engineering, after which he was returned to the front with a commission."

TO POPERINGHE
& RENINGHELST

DICKEBUSCH

POUR [illegible]

LA CLYTTE.

TO YPRE[S] ONTELE [illegible] MILES

SCHERPENBERG.

LOCRE

MT. KEMMEL

KEMMEL

NEUVE EGLISE.

BAILLEUL.

TO PLUG

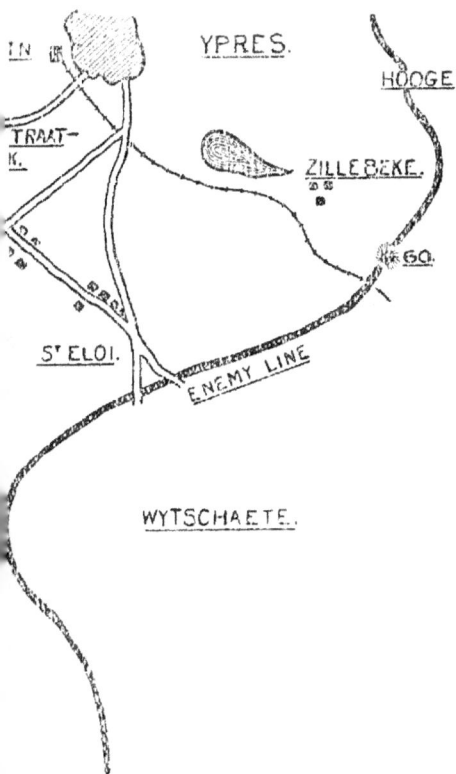

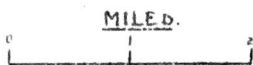

IN
YPRES.
HOOGE
TRAAT-
K.
ZILLEBEKE.
GO.
St ELOI.
ENEMY LINE

WYTSCHAETE.

N.

MILED.
0   1   2

CHAPTER XII

THE FURTHER PROGRESS OF THE WAR

It again becomes desirable to touch briefly on the further progress of the war as far as the events bear upon the scope of this narrative.

St. Eloi.—An action of considerable importance was brought about by a surprise attack of the Germans made on March 14th against the trenches east of St. Eloi. A large force of artillery was concentrated in this area under cover of mist, and a heavy volume of fire was suddenly brought to bear on our trenches in front of St. Eloi, the village itself and the approaches to it. There is a large mound lying to the south-east of the village. When the artillery attack was at its height a mine was exploded under this mound, and a strong hostile infantry attack was immediately launched against the trenches and the mound.

Our artillery opened fire at once, as well as our infantry, and inflicted considerable losses on the enemy during their advance, but chiefly owing to the explosion of the mine and the surprise of the overwhelming artillery attack, the enemy's infantry penetrated our trenches. As a consequence the garrisons of other works which had successfully resisted the assault were enfiladed and forced to retire just before it turned dark. A counter-attack was at once launched, and succeeded in recapturing much of the lost ground, but the mound remained in the hands of the enemy.

Hill 60.—This commanding hill, which afforded the enemy excellent artillery observation toward the west and north-west, was successfully mined and captured on the night of April 17th. During the night several of the enemy's counter-attacks were repulsed with heavy loss and fierce hand-to-hand fighting took place; but on the morning of the 18th the enemy succeeded in forcing back the troops holding the right of the hill to the reverse slope, where, however, they hung on throughout the day. On the evening of the 18th our men again stormed the hill, and the enemy was driven off at the point of the bayonet. On the 20th and following days many unsuccessful attacks were made by the enemy on Hill 60, which was continuously shelled by heavy artillery.

This was included in the area of operations of the 172nd Company immediately after it was taken (April 17-18th). The Germans seemed to attach great importance to its recapture, possibly because of its great value as an observation point, particularly in view of their attack, which, as it turned out, was now imminent. For this reason it was heavily shelled for a considerable period, and attack and counter-attack followed one after another. Battalions had to be relieved practically every twenty-four hours as casualties were very great. Our own guns seemed nearly all to have been moved away (in preparation for Neuve Chapelle, May 9th?). The whole area of approach from Wipers was kept under shrapnel fire.

In the meantime the Second Battle of Ypres had commenced.

On May 1st another attempt to recapture the hill was made, supported by great volumes of "poison gas," which caused nearly all the men along a front of about 400 yards to be immediately struck down by its fumes. The splendid courage with which the leaders rallied their men and subdued the natural tendency to panic, combined with the prompt intervention of supports, once more drove the enemy back.

A second and more severe "gas" attack, under much more favourable weather conditions, enabled the enemy to recapture this position on May 5th. The enemy's success was due solely to the use of "gas." It was only a few days later that means of counteracting this were put into force.

The Second Battle of Ypres.—The commencement of the battle was signalised by the enemy's first use of "poison gas" on April 22nd. The salient at that time was held on the extreme left by a French division (partly coloured colonial troops, Senegambians), the centre by a Canadian division, and the extreme right, including Hill 60, by a British division.

Thick yellow smoke was seen issuing from the

German trenches on the left, accompanied by a heavy bombardment.

What followed almost defies description. The effect of the gas was so virulent as to render the whole of the line held by the French incapable of any action at all. It was at first impossible for anyone to realise what had actually happened. The smoke and fumes hid everything from sight, and hundreds of men were thrown into a comatose or dying condition, and within an hour the whole position had to be abandoned, together with about fifty guns.

The left flank of the Canadians was thus left dangerously exposed, and a considerable force of Germans appears to have pushed in behind them and attacked their rear. Scarcely even realising what had happened, and in spite of the great danger to which they were exposed, the Canadians held their ground with a magnificent display of tenacity and courage; and it is not too much to say that the bearing and conduct of these splendid troops averted a disaster which might have been attended with the most serious consequences. Their losses were, however, appallingly high.

The Canadians were promptly supported by our reserves. Throughout the night the enemy's attacks were repulsed, effective counter-attacks were delivered, and at length touch was gained with the French right and a new line formed, but the position occupied by our men was seriously exposed.

General Foch informed Sir John French that it was his intention to make good the original line and regain the lost trenches. He asked the British to maintain their line, giving assurance that the original position would be re-established in a few days.

Fierce fighting with heavy casualties took place from April 23rd to 29th, the enemy using gas whenever the wind favoured him, but the British were able to substantially hold their ground, though in a very disadvantageous position.

In the meantime the French had only been able to make slight progress, and Sir John French was compelled to send instructions to Sir Herbert Plumer on May 1st to retire to a new line. This retirement was successfully completed by May 4th in spite of enemy attacks in the intervening days. It may be noted that Plumer had taken over the command of these operations and eventually took over the Second Army Corps when Smith-Dorrien returned to England.

Up to the morning of the 8th the enemy made attacks at short intervals, covered by gas, on all parts of the line to the east of Ypres, but was everywhere driven back with heavy loss.

Throughout the whole period since the first break of the line on the night of April 22nd all the troops in this area had been constantly subjected to violent artillery bombardment from a large mass of guns with an unlimited supply of ammunition. It proved impossible whilst under so vastly superior fire to dig efficient trenches or to properly reorganise the line after the confusion and demoralisation caused by the great gas surprise and the subsequent almost daily gas attacks. Nor was it until after this date (May 8th) that effective preventives had been devised and provided.

In these circumstances a violent bombardment of the centre of the salient broke out on the morning of the 8th, completely obliterating the trenches and causing enormous losses, but our men succeeded in holding the line.

On the 9th and 10th the bombardment and attacks were repeated and our line was forced back to some extent. A similar retirement resulted from heavy attacks on May 11th to 13th.

The enemy's losses were also heavy, but we had nothing like the artillery or ammunition the Germans had.

From the 13th the fighting died down until May 24th, when a violent outburst of gas against nearly the whole of the Ypres front was followed by heavy shell-fire, and the most determined attack was delivered against our position, and our line was again forced back to some extent.

As a result of the repeated enemy attacks the depth of the salient was reduced in the period from April 22nd to this date by two to three miles.

Battle of Neuve Chapelle—Festubert.—Operations were started in support of an attack by the French on May 9th. They achieved some success, but at the cost of serious casualties. The fighting ceased about May 24th.

CHAPTER XIII

MINING IN THE YPRES SALIENT

Situation.—From the time of the First Battle of Ypres in November, 1914, to the latter days of 1917, when it was flattened out by our advance, the Ypres salient, often simply known as *the* salient, though somewhat modified by the Second Battle of Ypres, formed roughly a semi-circle around the town.

It earned the reputation of being one of the most unhealthy parts of the line, and as the Boche held the higher ground, like the rim of a saucer, the enclosed area was open to continual observation. In the very early days troops could move along the roads, provided they were not in the immediate vicinity of the trenches, without much risk of being shelled as long as they were only in small parties, but by the early part of 1915 even the use of the Ypres — Dickebusch — La Clytte road was prohibited during the daytime as likely to draw enemy fire.

Up to February, 1915, a certain number of inhabitants had remained in Wipers, doing a thriving business as shopkeepers with the troops, but from that time on the enemy began shelling systematically, and there was hardly a day passed without one or more 17-inch shells (the real Jack Johnson) dropping there, when a tremendous black column of smoke and débris would rise, visible for miles. You could hear one rumbling through the air, from a distance of several miles, like a runaway tramcar.

As our front line had to be supplied via the town, in which the roads centred, this centre formed an attractive target for the enemy in his endeavours to disorganise transport.

Dickebusch was much the same up to about March, 1915, and from then on it was spasmodically shelled. Later on it became so unhealthy that no troops were allowed to billet there, and in June some huts were erected at the back of the village for the Sappers.

Owing to the shape of the salient the enemy could fire right across it and concentrate all his guns on any one spot.

Routine.—For by far the greater part of the time the Mole and his " opposite number," H. (later Lt.-Col., D.S.O., M.C.), were the only two officers in immediate charge of operations. At the beginning trips were made on alternate nights, leaving billets at dusk and returning at daybreak. Then, when something in the nature of dug-outs had been constructed, the officer going in would remain in for twenty-four hours. As it took something like three hours in and the same out, this meant a tour of duty of thirty hours and eighteen hours to rest and attend to other duties (see below).

Later trench duty alternated every two days, i.e. similar to above, fifty-four hours on and forty-two off. For example, leave billets for the trenches at seven, pick up fatigue and supplies at K.S.H., then via Voormezcele to St. Eloi and the trenches, relieving at ten. On duty till the same time, when relieved two nights later. Go out with outgoing party, and reach billets, say, 1 A.M. the next morning. The whole of that day free (*sic*), and start off again at seven the next evening. On arrival in the trenches most of the night was taken up by getting the new parties started on their work, but it was usually possible to get some sleep by morning; the same the following night. As there were usually several working places, one was kept busy seeing that no mistakes were made, direction and proper level adhered to, listening and checking reports. The responsibility was very heavy, as the danger of enemy operations was always present, and the safety of all the men, of the trench and its occupants depended on perpetual vigilance.

As a matter of fact the officer in billets also had a busy time, as he had to be practically company commander, adjutant, orderly-officer, sergeant-major and quartermaster all rolled into one. It devolved on him to arrange the working parties, requisition fatigues, secure supplies, make up records, grant local leave, deal with crimes, pay-roll, &c., and actually see that the fatigue party got started properly and took up the necessary timber, &c.

The men had more rest. They went in every third day, and, when in, worked in shifts. The day after their tour local leave would be granted to all who wanted it. The next day rifle inspection, &c., and that evening to the trenches for twenty-four hours.

Organisation.—For much of the time the party comprised two sections (one half-company), roughly one hundred men, so that there would be each night three working parties of, say, ten men and an N.C.O. each. Each party would be detailed to one working face (usually two faces going in **Q** and one in **R**). As the senior sub. (about three weeks' seniority in gazetting), H. was O.C. detachment, and as such had practically the full powers of a C.O. of a battalion.

Practically every pay-day brought forth its crop of " drunks," who had to be dealt with accordingly. One man was so uproarious that he was too much for the makeshift guardroom, and had to be pegged out on the ground until his violence abated. Pay-day usually came once a fortnight, when each man would draw fifteen francs, N.C.O.s in proportion. It took two or three days in succession to get all the men paid off, as some would be in the trenches. In some regiments the number of " drunks " made it necessary to restrict the issue of pay to five francs per month. The Royal Irish on more than one occasion celebrated the event by setting fire to their billets, to the accompaniment of crackling ammunition as the fire exploded it.

Later on various infantry officers and men (about fifty) were attached for instruction with the object of forming a mining section for each brigade; they were to learn to run short and shallow galleries for defensive and listening purposes. The Sappers themselves were "Army Troops," and as such stayed in one sector regardless of the movements of brigades and divisions.

Nominally the Sappers were under the command of the C.R.E. of the division occupying the sector, but in practice they were left with practically full discretion. As far as the ordinary staff were concerned, they looked on the miners as high priests of mystic rites.

Company H.Q. was originally at Bailleul. At that time Captain Johnson, V.C., was O.C. company. Later he was promoted to Brigade Major, and shortly afterwards killed by a sniper. Captain Hepburn (later Major, D.S.O.) then took over, and shortly after H.Q. was moved to Reninghelst. The other half-company, of whom little was seen, was mostly engaged in the vicinity of the Bluff. Originally O.C. company was a captain; later it became a major's command, and the O.C. section was often a captain.

The men were partly recruited from the infantry and partly specially enlisted. These latter were promised 6s. a day, and it was subsequently found to be without proper authorisation. This gave rise to a lot of trouble (see Diary, March 29th), when the position had to be explained. Eventually authority was obtained to recommend the most skilled men for the 6s. rate. A number of the specially enlisted men (sewer contractors, &c.) were over military age, and could not stand the hardships of active service, and so had to be discharged. Altogether they seemed to have been enlisted under misleading information, as many of them were under the impression that they would not be working in the area of shell-fire. Even those from the infantry (usually from coal mining districts) often preferred to be returned to their units, which was permitted. new-comers taking their places. Several of the officers attached for instruction also preferred to go back to their own jobs, as they found the general conditions of mining operations, often quite new to them, too trying.

General Programme.—The first job was to run the defensive gallery from R2, but this soon stopped. After the Boche blew in front of Q1 (April 15th), the most immediate job was to stave off the enemy with short defensive galleries A and D, " blowing " whenever he got close enough to be heard, at the same time sneaking around his works with our B gallery and driving for his trench and incidentally Snipers' House, a post which was a constant source of worry to our men. Why the gunners were not able to demolish it was never quite clear; possibly the difficulty was the great shortage of ammunition. Simultaneously C gallery was being driven for an exposed part of the enemy trench, hoping to be able to blow up a considerable section. As it ultimately turned out, the full execution of this project was blocked by the unexpected ramifications of the enemy defensive galleries, and it was only by *a space of hours* that another attempt on Q was forestalled. When we did blow (July 10th) it was seen from the explosions near the trench that the enemy had already started charging his mine, the charge being exploded by our own.

Later on, after Q1 had been connected to R1 by a sandbag parapet, E shaft was started. This was to be a deep-level shaft for the purpose of driving under all known or suspected galleries and blowing up the Mound. This was the beginning of the work which reached its fruition in the early part of 1916 with highly successful results. The Mound was then wiped out altogether, as well as a hundred yards or so of trench, and our infantry simply walked over and occupied the position. Unfortunately they were subjected to a concentrated bombardment, and the position could not be maintained. It was not till 1917 that this sector was taken, in the Battle of Messines or Wytschaete Ridge, June 7th.

Method of Operations.—It was found by experience that the ground over nearly all of the salient consisted of an upper bed of yellow clay about eight feet thick, underlaid by stiff blue clay, all more or less waterlogged. This was so much the case that trenches could only be dug a couple of feet deep, and the defences consisted chiefly of sandbag breastworks.

The R.E. knowledge of mining operations was very limited, being confined to a short course of instruction and some few explosion experiments with charges of only about ten pounds. It was found advisable to introduce a number of modifications based on mining experience. The charges were arrived at by empirical means. After selection of a suitable site the shaft would be started, and the mouth of the shaft protected by a dug-out built up of sandbags and covered. Dug-outs were also constructed for the men of the working party and officers, the dug-out for the latter also being used as storage for electrical instruments, fuse caps, &c. Explosives were either stored a short distance behind the trench or, when available later, in a magazine cut in the gallery.

The chief requisite for successful operations is secrecy. This meant that all signs of mining had to be concealed, and it was essential that no noise should be made while working. For this reason the clay was cut away with knife-edged " push-picks " rather than picked down in the ordinary way. The ground excavated was filled into bags, dragged back to the shaft, and hoisted by an "Armstrong" (*sic*) windlass. As the blue clay stained the bags a distinctive colour they also had to be concealed. Thus they could be built into parapets only if they were concealed by other bags.

Pumping had to be done by hand and almost continuously. Pumps were scarce and not very satisfactory. Sometimes a pump could be "salvaged" from a shelled village and put to mining purposes. One difficulty was that the hose would get punctured by shell fragments, and new hose could only be obtained by indenting for a whole pumping outfit. The hoisting and pumping was done as far as possible by infantry fatigues, the sappers only doing underground work, at the face, dragging bags back to the shaft, &c. The early shafts were twenty to twenty-five feet deep, later forty feet, and in the chalk soil of the Champagne district some were as much as two hundred feet deep. The ground required timbering all through, as it would not stand without support. There were two ideas of the Regulars which were proved to be mistaken : one, that it was impracticable to work through ground that had once been mined ; the other, that it was necessary to be underneath the enemy gallery to blow successfully. Provided there was enough cover between the gallery and the surface, a charge would exert its force in all directions.

There are two sorts of mining operations : the mine proper, which results in a crater on the surface ; or, using a smaller charge, the camouflet, which does not burst through to the surface. Unless it was intended to wreck some surface works, the camouflet was used for the destruction of enemy galleries. The purpose was not only to destroy his gallery, but also to force, if possible, the deadly gas from the explosion into his workings, and for that reason a crater was to be avoided. As the depth of the gallery below surface was, say, twenty feet, it was obvious that the enemy gallery would have to be within that distance to be wrecked by a charge that was not large enough to break through to the surface, and, of course, the nearer the more effective. The distance could only be guessed at by the noise heard—a difficult matter to judge. A stroke of a pick could probably be heard something like twenty to twenty-five feet away, while a sharp tap on timber could be detected still farther—up to, say, fifty feet. As far as circumstances allowed and as the distance could be judged, it was planned to get or to allow the enemy to approach within five feet. This was very nervy work. All operations would be stopped at suitable intervals for listening purposes. There is always some noise to be heard underground : the fall of a drip of water, a crumbling piece of clay, the creak of equipment through breathing, shells bursting on the surface, &c. It is, therefore, not surprising that men with every nerve strained to the utmost would report sounds of hostile mining which were not substantiated. While every such report was treated with respect, it would not be accepted unless confirmed either by H. or the Mole.

It added to our difficulties that the sound of tapping, even in the most certain cases, could only be caught sometimes at very long intervals. Altogether the mining game was rather like blind man's buff, with everyone blindfolded and depending on our ears for our lives and the safety of the trench. At the same time all reasonable risks had to be taken, as to "blow" without due cause meant revealing our own work to the enemy as well as wrecking our own efforts without any recompense. The Mole ventures to think that we never blew without inflicting serious damage on the enemy and knows that is not true of *his* operations.

Various listening devices, electrical microphones, &c., were submitted, but, whatever may have been perfected later, they were found useless, for they simply magnified the medley of different noises, while the ear could analyse the distinctive sounds and separate the characteristics of mining operations. No report of mining noises coming from other trenches was ever substantiated. Mostly it could be traced to men kicking their feet against the firing-step to warm themselves or some

similar cause, but each report had to be carefully
investigated, as one never knew what might be
coming. Naturally one got rather sick about it
sometimes, and H. once told an excited trench
commander he must have heard a wounded worm !
The experiences with the rats in R were a complete
deception for the time being.

. Ventilation was rather a problem. Small hand-
blowers with canvas or rubber hose were used, but
the ventilation was never good, and in some branch
galleries the air was so bad that only short shifts
could be worked. It was planned, for instance,
to drive a back-heading from the curve of B to
behind the trench to get a ventilation shaft.
Similarly a box-heading, so called from the style
of timbering, was connected by a pipe driven to
the surface to ventilate the Q workings. One could
sit there and listen to the ping of bullets passing
close to the spot where the pipe reached the surface.

It was some time before a satisfactory boring
tool was supplied. The first attempts were with
very expensive machined worms, very cumbersome
to handle, and consisting of a large number of
jointed pieces. Afterwards quite a simple augur
was used, not unlike a cheese scoop, with exten-
sion pieces. These were used for making listening
holes in advance of the gallery or for boring inclined
holes towards where we judged the enemy to be.
They made a hole about eight inches in diameter,
and some suitable canisters were made for insertion,

holding about fifty pounds each in a three feet canister.

The explosive used throughout was ammonal. N.B.—It was curious to note the descriptions of the mines fired before the Wytschaete Ridge attack. Not one of the half-dozen correspondents spelt ammonal correctly and each chose his own particular variant. It is a grey powder, put up mostly in tins like petrol tins, two tins of twenty-five pounds each in a wooden box. It is an aluminium-ammonium-nitrate compound, and very safe in handling. Nothing but detonation will explode it, but it must be kept dry, or else it will not fire. It has a speed of combustion between that of dynamite and black-powder, and was selected as being powerful but not too rapid, i.e. to give a comparatively slow heaving effect rather than a sharp rending.

On deciding to blow, the charge would be stacked against the face, all tins packed closely together and touching. An electric detonator, connected to leads (all connections carefully made and taped with rubber for insulation), would be inserted into the powder of one of the tins. Another common detonator, crimped on instantaneous fuse (orange coloured, and criss-crossed with thread so that it could be recognised by feel in the dark), would be inserted in another tin, and in the case of a large charge loose detonators were inserted in every third or so remaining tin, to be exploded by the general shock. The electric leads were run back to the shaft and surface. The fuse was only meant as a standby, and was only long enough to reach past the tamping so as to be accessible. To the end of the instantaneous fuse was spliced a sufficient length of time fuse to allow it to be spitted and then to reach the surface in safety. This was always put in, but on no occasion was it used. The only failure of electric firing experienced was on July 10th, when one of the subsidiary charges failed through a previous explosion having severed the leads and fuse.

In this connection one of the little jests of the men was as follows : occasionally a hand-thrown bomb of the jampot type would land with the fuse extinguished, in which case it could be lighted and returned to its original source. Some of the men amused themselves by stripping a piece of instantaneous fuse of its distinctive covering and substituting a piece of it for the usual short piece of time fuse in our own jampot bomb, and then throwing it *unlighted* at the enemy trench. The German would light it, thinking he could throw it back, but it would burst at once.

Having run the leads and fuse back as requisite, the tamping would be done. It is obvious that the explosion will seek the easiest path, and therefore one has to give the charge a solid backing or tamping to prevent it blowing down the gallery like a shot out of a gun. This tamping should be

one and a half times the distance of solid ground
to be broken through, i.e. for twenty feet, say
thirty-five feet of tamping. It was, however, not
always practicable to give it such a margin of
safety. Laying the tamping was a lengthy and
arduous job; filled sandbags, lowered from the
surface, had to be dragged in to the face and
stacked as tightly as possible. A tamped distance
of thirty feet would require the best part of a day's
work. Altogether the importance of making good
connections, &c., required the utmost care in
making preparations for a "blow" (all the
delicate work was done by one of the officers), so
that from first charging to actual firing might take
the best part of twenty-four hours, or in the case
of elaborate charges even longer. The most rapid
work was that of the camouflet of July 5th—two
hours. This was only achieved as something was
anticipated; leads were laid and sandbags stacked
all along the gallery before the necessity for action
arose. Furthermore, only a short tamping was
necessary, as a connection to the Boche working
was already established. Ventilation and pump
hose would be withdrawn before firing to avoid
damage from the explosion.

All preparations for firing having been completed and having warned neighbouring trenches
not to be alarmed, the officer in charge would
satisfy himself that all sappers were on the surface
and, where the charge was anywhere near the

trench, that the troops had been withdrawn, to avoid injury from possible toppling parapets, &c. The officer would then take the small hand magneto firing machine, give it a twist or two to excite the magneto, connect the leads, and then—" I hope those blessed connections are all O.K."—one twist of the wrist, accompanied simultaneously, so it seems, by the characteristic heave of the ground which answers that everything *was* O.K. and that the charge has fired. Another successful " blow " !

Even a fairly large charge in a camouflet makes curiously little noise, at the most a rumble, and even a crater only gives a dull roar; but the heave of the ground is unmistakable, like a young earthquake. In the case of a large charge the motion feels something like the combined roll and pitch of a ship in a short choppy sea. This heave can be felt at a distance of a mile or several miles, depending on the size of the charge. The troops in our sector became fairly used to it, provided they had due warning.

After firing, the ventilating pipe was dropped in the shaft, the blower started, and then, as far as that working place was concerned, a period of rest, twelve hours or so, to dissipate any gases that might have leaked through the tamping. This would then be tested by eventually lowering some small animal, in our case a rabbit, which otherwise led a luxurious life as the pet and mascot of the party. It ultimately came to an untimely end through an uninitiated officer shooting it with his revolver, which nearly caused a mutiny.

After testing the air one could enter the gallery again. The explosion would have wrecked and, near the charge, completely destroyed some length of it, and after extracting the tamping, which was usually slightly displaced but still largely intact, the wrecked portion would have to be driven anew only with rather more care, as the ground was completely shattered.

Guns, etc.—It may be well to explain that "whizzbangs" are the shells from field guns. Fired with a high velocity and low trajectory, the explosion follows almost simultaneously on the sound of the shell in flight. Howitzer shells, with their high angle, can be heard for some appreciable time before they burst, and are even visible as a black streak at the moment of falling to the ground. Armour-piercing or delay action shells are percussion shells with the fuse-plug in the base, and penetrate into the ground before bursting. They are used to destroy field works, but, except in the case of a direct hit, are comparatively harmless, as they smother themselves, though the shock of the explosion is rather alarming. The same is true of the minenwerfer or "sausage," a glorified bomb, which one can see wobbling through the air, and for that reason particularly upsetting, as it is difficult to judge where it will fall. They have a most destructive effect at the point of impact, being nothing but thin tubes packed with high explosive, but having no weight of metal to scatter about, the radius of destruction is very circumscribed.

From an examination of the German explosive found at Hill 60 it proved to be Westphalite, a low-grade dynamite compound, not too reliable in its action.

In conclusion the Mole wishes to pay a tribute to the steadfast courage and endurance of his "opposite number," H. It is a pleasure to state that he finished the war having won numerous decorations and repeated promotion, all of which was richly deserved.

LIST OF " BLOWS "

April 14.—Enemy, Q1.

May   3.—Our camouflet **A**.

,,   17.—   ,,   **A**.

,,   26.—   ,,   **D**.

,,   28.—   ,,   **A**.

June   5.—   ,,   **D**.

July   5.—   ,,   **C**.

,,   10.—General " blow " by us in all places.

,,   17.—Enemy, front of **E**.

,,   24.—Ours, C and cross-cut.

,,   25.—Enemy, right of C.

,,   28.—Enemy, between **Q** and Mound.

,,   30.—Our camouflet C.

,,   30.—Enemy, C.

,,   31.—Our camouflet C.

Aug.   1.—Enemy, T and two in C.

,,   2.—Enemy, C.

,,   3.—Enemy, front of **Q**.

CHAPTER XIV

DIARY ENTRIES

THE following "diary entries" under the respective dates are based on brief notes. Letters written
by the Mole are indicated as such. In some
instances amplifying notes are added.

The entries commence at Kemmel, shortly after
the arrival of the Mole (referred to as Lieut. G.)
there. H. and G. are instructed to take over work
at St. Eloi, a defensive mine started in a ruined
house in the remains of St. Eloi village.

TAKING OVER AT ST. ELOI

March 24, 1915.—Lieut. H. went to Dickebusch with Capt. Johnston and Lieut. G. to
arrange about billets. None available. 10 P.M.,
went to St. Eloi by foot to inspect site, returned
2.30 A.M. *Note:* this meant starting work while
still billeted at Kemmel, a considerable distance
and very inconvenient. All movement took place
at night, as much of this area (between St. Eloi
and Kemmel) was open to enemy observation by
day. There were no communication trenches in
those days.

March 25.—Lieut. H. to Dickebusch by foot
at 3.30 P.M. to see stores loaded and handed to
fatigue. (*Note:* Timber, sandbags, &c., collected
from R.E. dump at Dickebusch, and to be sent

to St. Eloi.) Met fatigue at 8 p.m. and took them to site. Started work. Returned. (*Note:* To Kemmel) 1 a.m.

[LETTER]

"*March* 26, 1915.

" We are at last getting settled down to work a little. We are billeted in our old haunts (K), but our own particular place is several miles north along the line, and it takes about two hours to reach it. Curiously enough, my old regiment has also gone up there, and I have already seen most of my old friends. M. and W. have taken over a working place to the south (they are the two who were with me), while I am acting as junior to the sub. who was already on the job. We all billet together, and have fairly decent quarters. Of course we are now in a much better position to make ourselves comfortable.

" The general programme of work is about as follows, subject to modification as necessity arises : A party of about fifteen men, with two or three N.C.O.'s, go up to the working place for a spell of forty-eight hours. They work in three shifts of eight hours, and billet in an adjacent farmhouse. My senior and I alternate leaving at dusk, marching up and spending the night supervising the work until it is time to return, getting in again just before dawn. We are fortunate in having comparatively good ground to work in, but some of the other places are very bad indeed.

" You will no doubt have received my card giving address as 172nd Company, Royal Engineers, Second Army. I got your last letter to the H.A.C.

" We have already had some interesting events. In one place the parapet of the trench started spewing sandbags into the shaft and practically filled it up. Fortunately no one was in it at the time. In another shaft quicksand began to come in and filled up the bottom. I don't know whether they can recover it. One of my fellow-officers got shot (killed) the other night through needlessly exposing himself in front of the trench. Two others lost their way and walked bang into the German lines, but got away without being spotted.

Last night, as the only officer in billets, a man was reported to me for striking an N.C.O.—a most serious offence on active service. Of course, I was absolutely unfamiliar with the proper military procedure, particularly as we never had an military crimes in the old regiment. However, I put him under arrest with a guard over him, which seems to have been the proper thing, and we held an investigation this morning. His mates back him up with a cock and bull story of the N.C.O. falling against a chair. I suppose the whole thing will go to a court martial.

" I met quite a number of my old comrades who

are now at the Artists' training school for officers, so it would seem as if pressure had been brought to bear on the colonel regarding commissions.

"Captain Johnson, V.C., does not believe in taking *unnecessary* risks, and has impressed us with the necessity of taking all due precautions, though, as a matter of fact, I believe he himself takes a good many chances. He reminds me somewhat of V. —a very soft-spoken sort of chap but as hard as nails. He is absolutely untiring and skips about all over the country as he has a large area under his charge. How he ever gets any sleep is still a mystery.

"The Germans have been firing pretty actively at night. The weather has been rather raw and cold again."

March 26.—Major N. G. and Captain Johnson arrived 7.30 P.M. Went to St. Eloi 10.20 P.M. with Lieut. G. Returned 3 A.M.

March 27.—Lieut. G. to St. Eloi with relief at 7.15 P.M. Major N. G. and Captain Johnson visited work at 9.30 P.M. and discussed methods. Lieut. G. returned 4.30 A.M.

March 28.—Lieut. H. to Bailleul at 12 noon. Returned with lorry to Diekebusch (*Note:* with timber) at 6.30 P.M. Later, took lorry to K.S.H. (*Note:* Kruisstraathoek) and met fatigue at 10 P.M.; then to St. Eloi. Returned 2.45 A.M.

March 29.—Major N. G. and Captain Johnson at Kemmel 10 A.M. Inquired into cases of men transferred at 6s. rate. Men voluntarily retransferred and agreed to stop on at 2s. 2d. rate.

Lieut. G. to St. Eloi via La Clytte, where he picked up lorry and timber. Left 7.30 P.M.

March 30.—Captain Johnson at Kemmel. Lieut. H. to Dickebusch with lorry and timber. No fatigue party as message had not been delivered to 85th Bde. Tried the Buffs—no good. Eventually obtained one from Northumberland Fusiliers. Reached trench 1 A.M.

Note: The supplies at that time mostly came from Bailleul (company headquarters), and were taken to K.S.H., at which point they had to be carried up by hand by a fatigue party. This was supplied by the infantry brigade occupying the trench. Fatigue parties were a constant source of annoyance and delay as they were often late, or assembled at a wrong place instead of the designated meeting-point, or failed to turn up altogether. In return the P.B.I. heartily cursed the Sappers as the cause of their blinkin' fatigues.

March 31.—Lieut. H. remained in trench all day.

Note: The practice had been to go up at dusk, and return, getting in before daybreak, but the long tramp from Kemmel to St. Eloi and back after a night in charge was very tiring, and as H. only got there at one in the morning he would on this occasion otherwise have had no time there at all.

Captain Johnson visited in the evening

Sapper King attached as orderly, left without orders and did not return to billets.

Lieut. G. went to K.S.H. to connect relief, fatigue and timber.

April 1.—Lieut. G. to St. Eloi with search-party for Sapper King, who was found; said he had lost his way and laid up behind trenches during day time. (*Note :* So he *said !*)

[LETTER]

" *April* 1, 1915.

" We have now two motor bikes between four of us, and may perhaps eventually get one apiece. They are Douglas twin-cylinder belt-driven machines with two gears and apparently quite useful machines. As none of us had ever ridden one, the trial trips were quite exciting and must have been very amusing for the onlookers. As I claimed to know most about it, I led the way, and, after looking the machine over to see what the various levers worked, I made my first attempt. Although not particularly graceful, it was quite successful. The others then followed, but each came quite a purler before they began to get the hang of it all. The machines showed marked signs of wear and tear by the time we stopped. They ought to be quite useful for running into town to get any little things that are necessary for the work, though I doubt if we can do much to utilise them in getting to our work.

" We had a nasty business at one of our working places. The Germans landed a trench-mortar bomb bang on top of it and killed one man and badly wounded three others. The shaft itself was not damaged, but the men were working over a refractory pump on top. Several others had at various times been wounded by ' strays ' on their way to or from the trenches. Last night was bright moonlight, very nice for walking, but rather too light for safety. I was leading a large party carrying timber up when one of the party had a bullet through his cap. I think it must have been a sniper as the report sounded very close. Fortunately no damage done.

" The men are mostly from the mining districts and have been transferred from line regiments. Thus I have a good many Royal Scots in my party. There are also some specially enlisted men who have worked for municipal corporations on sewers, etc., and they act as foremen. They are very useful men, but, as they have had absolutely no military training, they are quite unfamiliar with Army methods. That, however, is a minor (not miner) detail on this job. Of course one has many difficulties to contend with that would not occur on a " civvy " job. All timber has to be requisitioned, with much red tape, carrying parties arranged for, and, of course, all movement at night. The Brigadiers are kicking like steers at the large number of men required for these fatigue parties, but they are essential for carrying on the work.

" The men spend forty-eight hours in the trenches, where they have quite comfortable dug-outs, with braziers going. They work during this period four hours on and four hours off. After their spell in the trenches they have four days' rest, so they are not badly off—much better, I think, than the troops in the infantry."

April 2.—Lieuts. H. and G. to Bailleul and to see C.R.E. IIIrd Div. re St. Eloi second mine. To Dickebusch and K.S.II. per lorry. No fatigue arrived. Inspected site in R.B. trench (*Note:* later known as Q1) and returned.

April 3.—Lieut. G. takes up blower. Lieut. H. in, with small party for R.B. trench. Enemy shelled house (*Note:* where the mine was). Six casualties.

Note.—The new site in R.B. trench (Q1) was at the left end, just opposite the Mound, and, like the first St. Eloi mine, also in a house. Under close observation by the enemy from the Mound, and quietness and precaution necessary.

[LETTER]

" *April* 3, 1915.

" M. has just left for another section of the line, having been transferred to another company where they were very short of officers. W. remains here, but we expect to be leaving him before very long, as we are to move to different quarters. The address should, however, remain the same.

" I forgot to mention that I have a ' batman ' (Anglicé : servant) now who looks after my things. As far as work is concerned, we officers do rather more than the ordinary Tommy, as we are on the go most of the time—trench work at night, supervision of rations, inspection of arms, pay, roll calls, etc., by day. However, we manage to get a fair amount of sleep and do ourselves quite well with feeding, etc. In comparison with previous days, it is quite luxurious.

" One of our little jobs is, of course, the censoring of the men's letters. As they write most prolifically in an execrable hand, it takes some time. Some of the letters are quite weird, and the language is, as in their colloquial speech, red hot.

" Getting quite expert on the Douglas, though the roads are so frightfully bumpy that we do not go off except on business.

" Weather bright and clear, frosty at night."

We Start Operations

April 4.—Cellar cleaned out in R.B. trench and dug-out room sandbagged.

Lieut. G. looked for O4 trench to report on noise, but could not connect with guide. Returned at 1 A.M.

Note.—Cellar was full of rotten potatoes, and stank like ——. One room, fairly intact, was to be used as resting-place for the half of the working party that was off shift.

As for guide, he was not to be found. This was one of the frequent reports of " sounds of hostile mining," and one of us would have to turn out to investigate. If possible, it would be dealt with by the one on trench duty, otherwise, it fell to the other of us two, who was resting preparatory to the next tour of duty in the trench, so it was always highly unpopular.

[LETTER]

" *April* 5, 1915.

" The senior sub. (H.) is a very decent sort and very capable. He is a mining man from the **Straits** (tin), and only joined for the war. I believe **V.** and his regiment are not far away from us (to the **N.**), but do not know definitely. For all practical purposes we might be on opposite sides of the Globe.

" The N.C.O. assault case was dropped with a few days' arrest as there seems to have been considerable provocation. Still, if the Captain had carried it to a court martial the man would undoubtedly have had a very heavy sentence.

" We are starting a second working place, and it all keeps us tremendously busy. The alternation has proved rather a myth, and both of us have been out practically every night. We now propose alternately spending twenty-four hours in the trenches and will see how that works. We have had quite a lot of wet weather again.

" Pride goes before a fall! With the pavé as slippery as ice, the Douglas wagged her tail with a vengeance the last time I was out and I was on tenterhooks all the time. Skidded over several times, but was going slowly, so no damage was done.

" I am sorry to say we had some casualties from shelling the trenches the other night. They had been shelling along the line, and finally landed a crump next door to our working place; one man killed, one badly wounded and two bruised. Rotten luck, as it is really only about one chance in a thousand of their dropping near our particular places."

April 5.—Lieut. G. to Dickebusch to inspect billets and collect timber. Fatigue of Liverpool Scots two hours late. After G. inspected Nos. 1 and 2, listened in O4—nothing. Returned 4.30 A.M.

Note.—Original mine in St. Eloi designated No. 1 in trench R2, and subsequent forward mine designated No. 2 in trench Q1.

April 6.—Lieut. H. to Bailleul, returned 6 P.M. Visited St. E. Progress report. Returned 3 A.M. Heavy rain.

Note.—On return to billets a message was always written out stating progress of the work and any remarks, handed to orderly and sent to brigade signalling station, whence transmitted to company headquarters.

NEW BILLETS

April 7.—Moved to Dickebusch in the morning. Lieut. G. to trenches.

Note.—At last found habitable quarters vacant in Dickebusch.

[LETTER]

" *April* 8, 1915.

" Work progressing quite well under the circumstances, though it is bound to be rather slow. Here is a typical sort of day : up at 11 A.M., cup of tea, inspection of arms 11.30, an enormous breakfast at 12, in the afternoon pay roll and arranging for supplies. About two hours' rest to look at papers, etc. Dinner cum tea at 5. Left billets with two orderlies at 6 to walk to crossroads A, where saw timber unloaded from motor lorry (from headquarters) into wagon. Drove to R.E. park to pick up corrugated sheeting and sandbags, arrival at crossroads B, where all unloaded by 8.45. Fatigue party of seventy men supposed to meet me here at 9, but did not show up. At 10 left orderly No. 1 there, and proceeded up to the working places. Here a messenger caught me with a wire : ' Please inspect trench X, where they think they hear Germans mining.' No signs of fatigue party or stores. Returned to crossroads at midnight. Orderly No. 1 and stores vanished into thin air. By the way, all this in pouring rain. Left orderly No. 2 and proceeded alone to crossroads C, where eventually picked up guide for trench X. Went up there but could hear nothing at all. Returned and went back to crossroads B, where I now (3 A.M.) found both orderlies. The fatigue party had turned up at 11 and must have passed within fifty yards of us across the fields, but it was so pitch black that we had not seen them. Returned to billets, arriving 4.30 A.M., with daylight just appearing, very wet and just about able to shove one foot in front of the other. Sent in wire report. In bed at 5 A.M. Breakfast next morning very much in négligé. My senior had been just as busy as I on other things and had been howked out to look at another trench by Johnson (who may appear anywhere at any hour of the twenty-four), and did not get in very much earlier.

" Thank goodness, it is not always quite as strenuous as that, though it is quite a fair sample.

" We have now shifted into new billets, which are a trifle nearer the scene of operations. H. and I are now alone together. W. was left at the last place, where he is to be joined by another."

April 8.—Struck heavy flow of sewage, probably from cess-pit.

Note.—This was No. 1, which was running out under remains of houses in front of that part of the trench—firing trench—with the purpose of blowing up all cover if the enemy occupied them by snipers or otherwise.

April 9.—Lieut. H. to trenches.   No fatigue arrived.

[LETTER]

"*April* 9, 1915.

" I am writing to-night as I shall not have to turn out—the first time for a considerable period—unless I get some wire about visiting trenches. People are getting rather panicky about German mines, and we have had to investigate a number of stories of sounds of mining being heard—all of them without foundation as far as we are able to tell.

" I had to call on the C.R.E. (O.C. of the R.E.'s attached to the division) the other day.   I found he was the man who interviewed us about March 6, and, to my surprise, he recognised me at once, calling me by name.

" We see lots of ' Brass Hats ' now, as everybody is keenly interested in our work.   At night time practically anybody takes it upon himself to challenge figures in the dark.   I have got rather tired of being asked ' Who are you? ' and replying ' R.E.,' so I sometimes spring it first.   I shot my challenge the other night at two murky objects, and the reply was, ' Brigadier and Staff,' said staff apparently comprising one lone captain.   Very energetic of them, as they mostly are content to take reports on the state of the trenches without actually going up there.

" We are very comfortable in our new billets and hope they will let us remain here for some time."

April 10.—Lieut. H. stopped up. Lieut. G. to Bailleul, and saw fatigue started. Again in wrong place.

April 11.—Lieut. G. in and stopped up.

April 12.—Lieut. G. in. No fatigue—had to use sappers as carrying party.

April 13.—Lieut. H. went in. Double fatigue.

[LETTER]

" *April* 14, 1915.

" There is not much to write about at the moment, as I have already given you a pretty good idea of general conditions, and nothing special has since taken place.

" I hear the latest job going is that of dropping bombs from a kite, and suitable men are being sought. It doesn't sound very attractive to me, though exactly what it means is not at all clear.

" Things are quite lively along our section of the line just at present. There is an interchange of ' whiz-bangs ' by day, and a bit of ' rapid ' intermixed with machine-gun fire at night. Net result in most cases a lot of noise, and some more empty cartridge cases.

"Weather improving on the whole, but changeable.

"The Douglas is to my mind rather lightly built, though perhaps I am spoiled by good cars. Anyway, it has a great tendency to shed nuts, rattled off by the awful roads. I have indented for some spares, but don't quite know what I shall get."

The Enemy Strikes

April 14.—Lieut. H. stopped in.

No. 2 shaft completed. Enemy mine fired at 11.45. House and corner of trench blown in.

April 15.—Regarding mine exploded by Germans, probably from heading driven from a shaft in "snipers' house." Centre of crater about 50 feet short of our No. 2 house in **Q1**. Size of crater estimated 70 by 50 by 25 feet. House and 20 yards of trench collapsed. Sappers, 8 casualties.

April 16.—Lieuts. G. and H. up. Lieut. G. stayed in. Cleared away débris. Shaft slightly damaged. Lieut. D. C. arrived in evening.

A Wonderful Escape

Note.—The explosion shook the whole of the remains of the house down. Apart from sapper casualties, there were a number among the infantry, as part of the house was used as a strong point. Two men were working at the bottom of the shaft at the time, and it seemed certain that they had been killed. The infantry worked all night and cleared the débris away as best they could, rescuing the injured. In the morning they saw, with astonishment, smoke coming up. When the ruins were cleared away from the top of the shaft, it was found that the covering immediately over it had protected it, and the two men had escaped with a bad shaking from the shock, had climbed up and were smoking, and so eventually rescued.

H. was at **R2** when the enemy blew; at that time no dug-out at **Q1**.

[LETTER]

" April 17, 1915.

" Life continues pretty strenuous. After contending with a good many difficulties, we had things going comparatively smoothly. The lorry brought stuff out to our depot here. We finally acquired a wagon of our own to take it the next stage along. Fatigue parties had gradually been educated up to meeting us at the right place, and at something like the proper time. Then our troubles started all over again. The Germans exploded a mine close to our working place. Fortunately subsequent inspection showed that it did not cause much damage to our shaft. One man was killed and 10 others injured by falling débris. We were therefore shorthanded, and had in addition to clear away a tremendous amount of débris.

This we have done, and are now again in something like working order after a lot of unremitting hard work. We can consider ourselves jolly lucky that things were not far worse. Apparently they (the G.'s) had been going for the trench for some time, and, when they heard our work, stopped completely, firing the mine before they reached the trench in the hope of wrecking everything. It must have been a tremendous explosion, as I crawled out at night to see the crater—a cavernous hole 25 ft. deep, 50 ft. wide, and 75 ft. long. I guess at 500 lb. of high explosive. It so happened that neither H. nor I were actually on the spot when it occurred. At present it still means about 30 hours on, including getting to and from billets, and 18 hours off (such as it is) for us. We hope it will be easier soon. We have just been joined by a third man, who has yet to be shown the ropes. There is, however, some talk of still another working place, so his presence may not in itself mean much relief."

HILL 60

April 17.—Lieut. H. in. Attack by us on left, and mines exploded under German trench. Heavy shelling. Attack successful.

Note.—This was the capture of Hill 60.

[LETTER]

"*April* 20, 1915.

"In spite of the very strenuous times we have been having, I am very glad to be on this job.

Of course, we have far more work and responsibility than the subalterns in the infantry. In fact, we are exercising practically all the functions of a company commander.

" We have got our mine working again after heaps of trouble (I finished an absolutely continuous shift of 30 hours last night), as when we started drifting again the ground had all been so shaken by the concussion that it started running like sand. However, we are in good order again now. Did I tell you my theory? I believe our working saved the trench. The Germans had got their mine in to the point of explosion when we started the shaft. They heard us, and immediately stopped all work, and finally got so scared that they charged and fired where they were, without attempting to get under the trench. From their standpoint it must be regarded as a complete fiasco.

" I hear our people made a very nice little attack (successful) a night ago further along the line, taking Hill 60. Proceedings were inaugurated with blowing up German trenches. When the counter-attack was being repulsed, they turned two motor machine-guns on the close ranks of the Germans with deadly effect.

" Things are more like normal again now, and we propose working 24 hours in the trenches and 48 hours out, now that there are three of us on the job. We are to start a third working place,

but it will be possible for one man to cover all
three during his spell.   Our new man, **D. C.**, was
with the 9th Border (Pioneer) Regiment at home,
and is quite new to the trenches, so we are letting
him into it gradually.   His work has been largely
in Mexico.''

April 20.—Lieut. G. to Hill 60 to reconnoitre.
Returned 4 A.M. 21st.

April 21.—Lieut. H. in.   Lieut. G. to Hill 60.

[LETTER]

" *April* **23, 1915.**

" I have already mentioned **Hill 60.**   The
enclosed cutting from *The Times,* which you have
no doubt already seen, will refresh your memory.
As we have not enough troubles of our own, this
delightful health resort has now been added (only
temporarily we hope) to our area.   On the 20th
inst. Johnson suddenly appeared on the scene as
I was sitting down to breakfast.   I may here interpolate that I am at a place just off the map
(Dickebusch) and working at (St. Eloi).   He
howked me out, and we motored up to (Ypres).
From there we proceeded to 60.   (This is one of
the few places that can be reached in daylight, now,
that we hold the crest.)   We reconnoitred the
position, and made a choice of ground for carrying on our work.   We then returned to the town.
All this time the Germans, who have been strain-

ing every effort to retake the hill, were directing
a terrific bombardment against our front-line
trenches, as well as endeavouring to create a
' barrage ' of shrapnel between it and the town in
order to prevent supports being brought up and
also shelling the town. All kinds of guns were in
action, including the real Jack Johnson (their
17-in. howitzer). Words can hardly describe the
shelling—it was appalling! The sights in the
trenches were ghastly. Johnston, who has been
through it all since the very beginning, had seen
nothing quite as bad as their bombardment. We
had one narrow squeak; a ' crump ' (8-in. high
explosive) landed quite close, and had it exploded
would undoubtedly have wiped us out. Fortunately it proved to be a ' dud ' (i.e. did not explode)—one out of two ' duds ' in the four hours
we were up there!

"That night I took a party up to start work.
Lost our way, but by heading for the biggest
noise got there eventually. In the meantime
shelling had quieted down, but again revived to
such an extent that we had to take shelter under
a railway embankment for a couple of hours before
we could reach the trenches. On arriving there
we found that the position had in the meantime
again been captured. We were therefore unable
to accomplish our object, but I was able to put
the men on to useful work in the way of repairing
parapets and improving the trenches. I left them

there and ' hoofed ' back to billets, arriving 4 A.M.
What with walking about seventeen miles and the
general experience of the day I was ' bust to the
wide,' and thankful to get in.

" At noon (the 21st inst.) Johnson turned up
again, having had a wire report from me. We
selected another position from sketches and knowledge of the ground. In the evening I took D. C.
(our new man) with me, and we went by motor
lorry to the town, picked up our party, got them
up and at work. We withdrew the charges from
a captured German mine. We then returned per
feet and lorry to billets—arrival broad daylight,
4.30 A.M.

" Next night I went up to our own place for a
spell to give H. a relief. It is pretty strenuous,
and I do not think we can carry on this new work
in addition to our own for more than a few days.
Johnston is very fed up about it.

" *The Times* leader as to not over-estimating
local successes is much to the point.

" Hope to get a real rest to-night, but D. C.
(who will probably carry on with the Hill) and H.
are busy again.

" Our men on the Hill were splendid. They
were hanging on tooth and nail in spite of the
terrific shelling."

ATTACK EXPECTED AT ST. ELOI

April 22.—Lieut. H. went up with explosive.

No fatigue. K.S.H. shelled 10.45 P.M. Rang up Brigade and had fatigue turned out.

Note.—It was important to get explosives up to St. Eloi that night as prompt action might be necessary.

Lieut. D. C. to Hill 60, but turned back by Brigadier owing to uncertain position and French reverse on left.

April 23.—Lieut. H. stopped up at Q1 as party reported noises, and Brigadier asked that confidence should be restored. Prepared for charging mines. Attack expected. Telephoned R2 to prepare for charging.

(*Note.*—This was during the day. Movement between Q1 and R2 could only be effected during darkness as it meant walking in full view of the enemy trenches and the Mound.)

Went to R2 at 7. Charged heading and put in tamping.

(*Note.*—The Mole had received an urgent message about 4 A.M. to order the small party of sappers billeted in Ypres to leave at once, presumably on account of expected shelling, and to attach themselves to Dickebusch section. Dashed up there on motor-bike and gave necessary instructions.)

Lieuts. G. and M. took over **Q1** and **R2** respectively.

(*Note.*—Lieut. M. just arrived.)

Lieut. H. returned to billets 11.30 P.M.

G. and M. report all ready for firing if required.

Possible Withdrawal From St. Eloi

April 24.—Both mines ready and standing by.

Lieut. D. C. to Hill 60. Returned—turned back by Brigadier.

Lieut. H. took over at Q1, and an N.C.O. in R2.

[LETTER]

April 25, 1915.

"We are very busy, chiefly because of the authorities are undecided as to what they want to do, and there is a lot of chopping and changing about."

Carry On!

April 25.—Lieut. H. up. Started work in Q1 again. R2 standing by.

Note.—The charge was in the face of the heading, stopping further advance, and, as a matter of fact, this heading never was driven further. In Q1 the charge had been put in a chamber cut in the side and was left there, but the heading could be and was advanced.

Lieut. D. C. to T2, listening.

Lieut. G. standing by for Hill 60 (*Note :* with a ton or so of ammonal to blow up the captured mine if it appeared that the enemy would re-capture it.)

April 26.—Lieut. M. in. Advance in Q1. R2 standing by.

Lieut. G. standing by for Hill 60.

Lieut. H. listening in T2.   Nothing.

Lieut. D. C. relieved Lieut. M. in Q1 at 9 P.M.

April 27.—Lieut. H. relieved Lieut. D. C. in Q1.

Lieut. G. to Hill 60.

Note.—To prepare captured mine for our own offensive purposes.   After this the procedure was for a working party and supplies to go by lorry to Wipers station and unload there.   A fatigue party then picked up and carried to the Hill (by this time known as " Murder Hill ").   The fatigue was supplied by reserve troops of a local brigade, billeted in dug-outs in the railway embankment near Zillebeke Lake ; Brigade H.Q. near Zillebeke.   The route was usually from the station and following close to or on the railway line.   The whole of the route was much exposed and the approach to the Hill particularly bad.   This was in a gully which was subjected to frequent searching bursts of shrapnel, and it was necessary to move as quickly as could be conveniently managed to the entrance to the communication trench which ascended the steep hillside.   At the bottom of this were some dug-outs and the headquarters of the infantry occupying the trenches.   (To the right was the Bluff.)

Carrying parties necessarily move slowly, and there was hardly one occasion where there were not one or more casualties amongst either the sappers or the fatigue party.

April 28.—Lieut. M. relieved Lieut. H. in **Q1**.
Lieut. D. C. to Hill 60 and returned.

[LETTER]

April 28, 1915.

" Our operations continue very unsettled on account of the general situation up here and it continues to keep us very busy.   One cannot get away from the fact that the Germans have given us a very nasty smack, no matter how the papers try to gloss it over."

April 29.—Lieut. H. relieved Lieut. M. in **Q1**.
Lieut. G. to Hill 60.

ENEMY MAKES ANOTHER ATTEMPT

April 30.—Doubtful as to noises heard.
(*Note :* Must refer to reported noises heard in **Q1** mine.)

Lieut. M. relieved Lieut. H., 10 P.M.
Lieut. D. C. to Hill 60.   Stopped up.

GAS

[LETTER]

" *April 30, 1915.*

" A good deal is being written about the asphyxiating gas now, so it is of interest to state what we know about it.   It has been identified as chlorine, and is turned loose from cylinders in the German trenches through short pipes pointing towards our lines. They depend on the wind to carry it to us. It is undoubtedly very disagreeable and irritating, as it causes much irritation of the throat, coughing and streaming eyes, to say the least of it, and if inhaled in quantities may be dangerous. We are informed that there are several simple remedies; even an ordinary wet handkerchief over the mouth is said to obviate most of the danger.

" The line runs in almost a three-quarter circle around Ypres, and thus forms a salient subject to attack from three sides, the centre (the town), through which most of the supply roads pass, being, of course, particularly attractive as a target. Any serious reverse on one of the flanks would mean the withdrawal of all that portion in order to straighten our line.

" Hill 60 was very valuable to the Germans, as it gave them a certain amount of command over the interior of the circle, and from that same standpoint is of value to us. For offensive purposes, however, it is not particularly important.

" We continue as busy as ever."

May 1.—Lieut. G. to Hill 60. Relieved Lieut. D. C. (*Note:* Most of this time the enemy was shelling heavily, and was trying to use gas whenever the wind favoured.)

Enemy Getting Closer.

Lieut. H. went up to Q1 as noises were reported again. Took up 100 lb. explosive. Tapping heard once quite close, and afterwards at intervals far off.

May 2.—Lieut. M. took over at 11 P.M. Brought up boring tool. Work at Hill 60 finished.

Note.—On the night of May 1st, as the party arrived in the gully there was a succession of shrapnel bursts. The whole party was thrown into confusion. The Mole got his own sappers into dug-outs, and then looked after the men on fatigue (nominally under their own officer). There were 11 casualties altogether, and in the darkness he dragged those he could find into the best shelter available. All this time the shrapnel was continuing. Fortunately most of it bursting fairly high, but he could feel fragments falling like hail. (This was before the days of " tin hats "). Most of the fatigue party had disappeared, and it was stated afterwards that they retired with the belief that there was some order to that effect, which was incorrect.

The Mole had previously been informed that the situation on the hill was very uncertain, and he was to report to the O.C. Camerons at their H.Q. He did so, and eventually, after about an hour's wait, decided to proceed. This was when it was found that the fatigue had dispersed. The subaltern in charge was very upset, both by this and by the casualties his party had sustained, but by making two trips the most necessary of the supplies were got up.

Altogether everybody was thankful eventually to hand over to another company, by which time the enemy's activity temporarily had abated.

We Frustrate The Enemy

May 3.—Lieut. M. listened all day. Put in bore 6 feet deep when noises were again heard quite close and underneath. Instructed him to fire 100-lb. charge in the face. Charge fired 3.15 P.M. Noises heard up to last moment.

Lieut. H. went up and started Lieut. D. C. in R1 (new site for a shaft). At Q1 found shaft blocked with débris.

[LETTER]

"*May* 4, 1915.

" With regard to the enemy's shelling, the number of ' duds ' varies a lot—sometimes practically all effective, and at other times as many as 50 per cent., and occasionally as many as 75 per cent., are 'duds,' but as a general rule most of them burst. Shrapnel, however, is not really dangerous unless it bursts fairly close and low down; otherwise, if having any effect at all, those within radius of fire get only slight wounds or bad bruises. High-explosive (percussion shells) are very erratic, and though fragments may in isolated cases be thrown surprising distances, particularly

if any brick-work is struck, the general effect is
very local and confined to a small radius. Shrapnel
can be viewed with comparative indifference from
the shelter of trenches, though very unpleasant
out in the open. On the other hand, high explosives make a bad mess landing on a parapet, but
are very unlikely to do you any damage out in the
open, as the chances of a direct hit are so small.

About the most unpleasant thing is the big
trench-mortar bomb (Minenwerfer), which has
practically all the explosive effect of an 8-in. crump
(though without its weight of metal), but can be
landed with greater accuracy on a trench. I can
write with some authority on these points, as in connection with the work on 60 I have had experiences
with them all under the different conditions. I
may add here that last night I handed over that
working place to another company, and so hope
to have seen the last of it. It has been a pretty
warm spot for everybody concerned. Now to
revert to past events.

" After my first visits up there the local situation was so uncertain that falling back was quite
on the cards, and for 48 hours I ' stood by ' ready
to let off a charge of over a ton of high explosive !
If the Germans had come on then to our trenches
they would never have known what struck them.
Eventually it was decided to carry on, and a
listening gallery (to listen for hostile mining) was
run out ; when this was completed I handed over.

" Every time I went up there we had some excitement. On one occasion I got caught in a perfect rain of shrapnel, which lasted almost continuously for 15 minutes, while I flattened myself up against my old friend the railway cutting. Neither I nor my orderly were injured at all, though fragments were rattling all round and occasionally on to us. Another time on arriving I found over half the people in the trenches overcome with gas. Fortunately the wind swung round, and I think the Germans got a taste of their own medicine. It certainly is vile stuff and very dangerous, though respirators (of which I have one) are something of a protection.

" I hear the French are going to use ' turpinite,' which is supposed to give off a perfectly deadly fume when it explodes. Taking it altogether our parties up there were very lucky, though we had a number of casualties.

" In the meantime in our proper district we have had an interesting time. We heard Germans countermining, slipped in a charge and fired, with what we hope are successful results. We think we have wiped that particular lot out, and we certainly have spoiled their little game. No doubt this all sounds very vicious, but after seeing the way our people have suffered in one way or another, I am out to do the Germans in any way I possibly can.

" The old county regiments, which really form

the backbone of the Army and which hold the trenches round here, stick it to the last, but the casualties have at times been appalling. The Germans, I think, have been at least as badly hit.

" We believe that the Germans, with their new formations, are now at their highest possible strength and can continue the necessary reinforcements to maintain it for about three months. After that they should be steadily on the decline. The French should continue to gain strength slightly, and we, of course, have all of Kitchener's army yet to come. I hear, however, that the later officers of K.'s army are in many cases simply awful—far below standard; don't know anything, and don't much care to learn—simply joined to sport khaki at home. I often get very hot when I think of the many good men out here aching to take commissions but blocked by some d—— fool C.O.

" Johnson has left us; got a staff job as Brigade Major, a big step for him. As he is a professional soldier it means quite a lot to him, and for his sake we are very glad of it, though sorry to lose him. Our present C.O. (a very decent chap) is of the same class as ourselves—miner and ' temporary,' but whether a Regular will be put in over his head remains to be seen.

" As you may perhaps have already guessed from the length of this letter, this is a ' night off '— the first for ' many moons.'

" The weather is getting quite hot."

Hostile Mine Suspected

May 4.—Cleaned up **Q1**.

Lieut. D. C. reported noises in **R1** of sapping. Instructed him to sink pit for use of boring tools. Went over there at dusk and heard tapping. Sent for boring tool. Lieut. G. took over in **Q1**.

Lieut. H. to **R1**.

May 5.—Tried boring machine, but it would not clear in sandy clay on a down hole. Sank pit as shaft 6 ft. Noises faint. Much grenading. (*Note:* Rifle-grenades.)

Lieut. G. to **Q1**.

Lieut. D. C. took over in **R1**.

Rats !

May 6.—Lieut. D. C., **R1**, reported noises were traced to rats at 8 A.M. (*Note:* A nest of rats was found in the parapet. They had made a noise exactly like the tapping of mining operations.)

Lieuts. G. and H. took over at 10 P.M.

May 7.—Lieut. H. to **T1** to listen for reported noises. Moved all men away and heard nothing. Work progressing in **R1** and **Q1**. Lieut. M. took over both places at midnight. Lieut. D. C. left for Kemmel.

[LETTER]

" *May* 7, 1915.

" D. C. leaves us for another sector, but a third man, M. (a Canadian), remains with us, which should help. Nevertheless, very busy as before."

May 8.—Lieut. M. wounded by rifle-grenade (R1), also two other sapper casualties. Lieut. G. took over.

May 9.—Order to lay leads to Q3 in case of retirement. Lieut. H. took over.

[LETTER]

" *May* 10, 1915.

" While life continues full of events, there is not a great deal to write about as it is largely a repetition of previous experiences, standing by with the possibility of a shift, etc. We have, however, carried on with our work. Our third man, M., has been slightly wounded by a rifle-grenade and is now in rest camp, so we are again down to two officers, with rather more work on our hands than before. The work is not without its humorous sides. We have been solemnly called out to listen to ' sounds of hostile mining,' which proved to be a couple of bull-frogs in front of a trench. On another occasion a nest of rats was found to be the cause of disturbance. Several times people stamping their feet somewhere along the trench have caused unnecessary alarm, and, what to us is still more annoying, a rush trip to some outlying trench by one of us to investigate. Hence frequent loud curses !

" I think I have at last found out why the Germans were so furious when we originally took Hill 60, as has been shown by their persistent efforts ever since. I believe they were intending their big attack on the left and wanted to use it as an observation point. This, of course, was spoiled by our action. At present I hear the Hill is ' no man's land,' a ghastly wreckage of craters, shell-holes and corpses.

" The average officer's (infantry) knowledge of technology is distinctly weak. I have been much amused by perturbed inquiries as to what would happen if any projectile landed on the exploder (magneto) box which we keep in the trench to fire the charges. Apparently they think it is itself highly explosive! I once found that my instructions to a sentry that no one was to touch it had been supplemented by an O.C. trench to the effect that no one was to go *near* it!

" The *Lusitania* outrage is terrible, but not surprising, as it is simply on a par with many of their other deeds. I trust none of our friends were on board."

⌈LETTER⌉

" *May* 15, 1915.

" Re gas, we all keep respirators ready for immediate use. They have not tried it here so far. The conditions have to be just right for them to use it or they may find it disastrous for themselves. At Hill 60 only a few of our R.E. men were slightly gassed, I am glad to say. Most of us favour retaliation in any form that can be devised.

They are certainly out to use any destructive agency they can, and will apply anything they have regardless of what we may or may not do.

"I did not think the *Lusitania* outrage would bring the Americans in, but for Wilson to talk the absolute drivel he does is simply sickening.

"The explosive we use, ammonal, is pretty safe stuff, and will even stand a rifle bullet fired into it without exploding. It would, however, probably go off if a shell landed directly on a box.

"We are quite satisfied with our present C.O., but I hear that we are practically sure to have a 'Regular' put in.

"We had a flying visit from Empire Jack last night. He seemed satisfied but rather subdued, having fallen into a hole full of water up to his waist!

"During M.'s absence (rest camp), H. and I are working straight alternate shifts, 30 hours from billet to billet and 18 off. As you have to catch up lost sleep, feed and attend to routine matters in billets, arrange supplies, etc., during the 18 hours off, it does not leave many spare minutes."

Awaiting Our Opportunity

May 15.—Lieut. H. took over at **10.30.** Sounds reported in 1A (*Note:* **Q1**) at **11** P.M. Estimated distance over **15** ft. Resumed work quietly.

May 16.—Stopped work in 1A at 10 A.M. Sounds closer, about 10 ft. Put in two 4-ft. listening holes. Carried on 1B. Germans worked steadily all day until 7.30, when they stopped until 12 P.M. Lieut. G. took over at 10.30 P.M.

We Counter The Enemy
May 17.—Lieut. G. reported sounds clearer at 7.30 A.M. Charged and tamped. Fired at 3.30 P.M. A little smoke seen in old crater. (*Note:* German crater, see April 15.) Strong heave, but did not blow through. (*Note:* To surface.)

May 19.—Lieut. H. reconnoitres and arrested by Lincolns.

[LETTER]

"*May* 20, 1915.

" We have again been able to administer a lesson to the Germans. We heard them mining from one of our headings, and promptly prepared a nice reception for them. We loaded up our heading with 200 lb. of ammonal, and then put in partial tamping (filled sandbags) so that we could continue listening. We waited until they began to get close, completed the tamping, and then fired. I had the pleasure of working the exploder myself. The ground gave a heave like an earthquake, which was felt for some considerable distance around, but very little débris was thrown in the air, so we must have scuppered them all right—

200 lb. is a pretty heavy charge. We hope we have ruined their gallery for some distance back, to say nothing of wiping out the working party, while our own gallery, protected by the tamping, is comparatively little damaged. I consider we are now two up on them, as their original effort may be considered as all square, and we have now successfully brought off two of these little pyrotechnical displays. I fancy they must be feeling rather preoccupied and slightly nervous.

" Rather a curious thing happened further down the line where some of our company are working. They had a similar successful experience, which evidently worried the Germans very much. The trench was held by some newly arrived Territorials, quite green. The enemy bombed a bit, and the terriers turned tail and fled without giving the miners any warning. The latter came up for something, and finding the trench deserted, also, quite properly, hopped off. Then a small German patrol came over, looted the trench, pinching field-glasses, etc., left behind, and also tried to blow up the shaft. Finding the trench evacuated, the Germans brought over some of their cheap and nasty explosive, very poor dynamite, which I identified as Westfalit at Hill 60. Fortunately, in spite of their putting in fuse and detonators, the stuff failed to go off, so that the shaft was undamaged. Later our people peacefully resumed occupation of the trench, the patrol having retired. I suppose the Germans feared some hidden mine.

" The whole thing is extraordinary, and the Germans must have feared a trap. The terriers must be feeling highly ashamed of themselves, for the Germans now hang out taunting signs : ' Come on, you " Fighting Tigers," ' etc., for I believe the particular regiment style themselves with some such high-flown title. No doubt they will steady down in future.

" We hear our third man, M., has been transferred from rest camp down to the base, so I suppose we shall not see him again for some time at least. This means we shall have to continue with just the two of us. Our programme has been about as follows : I, for instance, come in after a day in the trenches about midnight, have a hasty supper, and get to bed to sleep till noon, catching up lost sleep as far as possible. Then breakfast at noon, and the afternoon almost wholly occupied with routine matters. A hasty dinner at 7, and then off to the trenches for another 30 hours' spell. We are now going to experiment with spending 48 hours in the trenches, so that the man ' out ' has something like one clear day. Of course, one gets a certain amount of sleep up there—we have quite a decent dug-out—but it is very broken, and usually only for a few hours, as there is almost always something that wants attention.

"I forget whether I ever told you that the company consists of four sections, of which we have two here. There is some talk of concentrating them all here in the future.

"The C.R.E. makes a daily round of the various R.E.'s under his control, and usually looks in to see the one of us who is here about noon every day. We have a chat, and hear the latest news."

[LETTER]

"*May* 22, 1915.

"We hear some of K.'s Army are arriving at last.

"Out here we all know that the ammunition supply (shells, and particularly H.E.) is far too scanty. Not only that, but the guns are getting very worn, and consequently inaccurate. One of the standing jokes is 'the ascendancy of our artillery,' much quoted in official and semi-official statements—a grim jest to the men in the trenches! I only hope that people at home will wake up in earnest. For practical purposes you might almost say the war has only just started.

"It is necessary to keep hammering home the fact that the united resources of the country *must* be brought to bear on the war. Kitchener had his hands too full with organising the New Army, and could not devote the time to munition supplies as well.

" The Press generally puts too rosy a complexion on local victories and glosses over defeats. A look at the map shows what progress we have made in the last six months.

" The German communiqués are by no means to be despised.

" I consider the Germans are beaten now, but it is going to take a lot of hard fighting to convince them of it, and render them unable to start a conflict like this again in a few years' time."

The Enemy Tries Again

May 22.—Lieut. H. in. Heard Germans advancing in Q1 main heading. Put in small 6-ft. heading, and then stopped and got charge down.

May 23.—Germans coming on, but very slowly and suspiciously. Lieut. G. took over at 10 P.M.

Watchful Waiting

May 24.—Lieut. G. reports Germans working slowly.

May 25.—Working slowly and steadily. Lieut. H. took over at 11 P.M.

[LETTER]

" *May* 26, 1915.

" My remarks on Wilson's speech referred to the ' too proud to fight ' portion.

" Empire Jack has no doubt done quite a lot of

useful work in stirring the authorities up and getting the thing started.

"I am really keeping quite fit, though it is something of a strain all the time. I usually manage to get quite a good sleep and rest when the opportunity offers—rather emulating the camel. In the words of the popular saying, ' A camel can go eight days without a drink—but who the h—— wants to be a camel? '

" There has been a lot of rot talked about the *Daily Mail's* article on Kitchener. On the whole, I thought it quite sensible, and it seems to have brought matters to a head.

" I saw W. M. for a few minutes to-day. He is in one of the mining companies, but at present several of them, which are in rather an embryonic condition, are attached to the other half of our own company, and are to undertake a rather larger and more extensive effort on our left. In the meantime H. and I are pegging away steadily around St. E. As you know, we amuse ourselves at intervals with counter-mines which keep the Germans busy (there is another one to be expected shortly—they are very persistent) and in the interval make progress in another gallery.

" One of our institutions is a rabbit which we lower down the shaft after a blow up, having allowed a suitable time to elapse. This is to test the air, as a lighted candle gives no indication of fumes from explosive.

" I believe quite a number of mining people are getting commissions now, and one of the latest schemes is to attach a mining officer to the brigade. It will be his job to investigate scares of hostile mining and allow us to stick to our proper work. This is all to the good, as it means that people with special knowledge are gradually being used to the best advantage.

" The weather is quite hot at present. I wonder if we are in for another scorching summer to counterbalance the awful winter we had? "

Still Another Effort

May 26.—New German heading heard in 1D. Put down 11 ft. borehole and charged with 70 lb. Tamped heading solid. Fired 8.35 P.M. Probably successful. Heavy heave.

May 27.—Got into 1A and B at 5 P.M. and placed listener.

Lieut. G. took over at 10 P.M.

May 28.—1A charged and fired 200 lb. at 4 P.M. Some smoke and flame over crater. Men report rumbling noises heard from shaft for one hour afterwards.

[LETTER]

" *May* 80, 1915.

" We have again been successful in countermining the Germans. This is very satisfactory in its way but delays our work of going for their trench.

"People seem to be waking up at home and there is now some reason to believe that *England will abandon her neutrality.*

"The weather is very changeable. One day is absolutely broiling out in the sun ; the next is distinctly raw and chilly. This makes it rather difficult to dress suitably, particularly as we now go up to the trenches for two days. On the whole, this arrangement is more satisfactory. Unless things are very urgent, such as supervision of the charge when about to blow up the Germans, we simply take time for a decent sleep, say, six hours, in the dug-out in the fire trench. It was impossible to continue indefinitely as we were doing.

"I always wonder when about to turn the exploder whether all the joints, detonators, etc., are all right, and am relieved when I feel the heave of the earth under me as the charge goes off."

More Interruptions

May 31.—Lieut. H. in ; Germans heard, estimated 15—18 ft. off at 6 P.M. Lieut. G. relieved at 11 P.M.

June 1.—No noises heard to-day.

June 2.—Noises heard again fairly close. Lieut. H. took over. Trouble with fatigue.

June 3.—Sounds heard all day. Sounds close at 11 P.M. Got ready to charge bore-hole.

[LETTER]

"*June* 4, 1915.

"There is not very much in the way of news; nothing startling to relate, which is perhaps just as well. Our work progresses steadily, though naturally very gradually.

"The country round here is really quite attractive now. It is astonishing how crops have grown, considering we are only about three miles from the firing-line, as the crow flies; it seems about ten on a pitch black night when the clay is as slippery as ice and it takes at least a two hours' struggle to get there. Fortunately this is the case much less frequently now, though during the winter months those were the prevailing conditions. It is a wonder how the fields have been ploughed and crops sown. I certainly don't recollect ever seeing anyone work at them, but the wheat is shoulder-high.

"H. and I lead a funny sort of Box and Cox existence. We only see each other for a few minutes every two days, when we relieve each other in the trenches.

"We have seen a Zeppelin on several occasions, either at dusk or dawn, but well within the German lines and out of gun range. I believe our aeroplane men had a whack at it, but have not heard of any results."

June 4.—Sounds all day, but only distinct in the evening. Lieut. G. relieved at 10 P.M.

June 5.—Fired 150 lb. camouflet in 1D at 5 P.M. Heard quite close, and men say could hear tin rattle.

[LETTER]

"*June* 8, 1915.

" We have again fired a counter-mine. Otherwise there is not much new.

" Some of K.'s Army are here, and are being mixed in with other regiments for their initiation into trench warfare. It is rumoured that some of the troops who have been at it for a long time are to go down to bases for a rest. They certainly all deserve it. It is very wearing work for everybody, though, of course, weather conditions are so much better now.

" Rather an amusing thing happened when I fired our charge this last time. We usually warn trench commanders in the vicinity, so that there will be no undue alarm when the ground gives a heave, as it does for hundreds of yards around. This was also done in this instance, but a party of men who were doing some digging in a communication trench were not told of it. They were rather new, and when they felt the shock they grabbed their rifles and trained them on to the ground, thinking someone was coming up from beneath!

"We are kept so busy blocking the German mining that our actual progress is very slow. So far, however, we have distinctly the better of them."

THE ENEMY PERSISTS

June 8.—Lieut. H. in. Germans again heard somewhere south of **A** and east of **B**. Borehole put down in end of **A**. Lieut. G. took over at 10.30 P.M.

June 9.—Nothing heard except faint sounds.

June 10.—Faint noises. We shelled the Mound with 28-6 in. in afternoon. (*Note :* Necessitating temporary withdrawal from **Q1**. Quite a respectable shoot for our gunners in those days. Conducted with great ceremony.) Lieut. H. took over **10.30**.

[LETTER]

"*June* 11, 1915.

"I have not heard of gas being used by us so far.

"We were all very sorry to hear that Johnson was killed a few days ago.

"Maude's article was quite interesting, though I do not agree with all his views. I consider an enormous supply of H.E. shells is most important, and though not a universal panacea, probably the most important single factor in the present stage of the war. Shrapnel is about as effective as spray from a watering can. You will remember I wrote some time ago about these various shells. Another thing we want badly is a supply of trench howitzers, to say nothing of many more machine-guns. Hand grenades are now more plentiful than they were. The very heavy artillery (15-inch and mythical 21-inch) are of precious little value at present, though no doubt necessary if we ever got to the point of attacking real fortresses."

A False Alarm?

June 11.—Heard nothing. Relief late, owing to going via new communication trench.

June 12.—Heard nothing for certain. Lieut. G. takes over.

June 13.—Cross-cut west started in 1A, plus three boreholes.

June 14.—Heard them again between A. and B. Lieut. H. takes over

Wind Up

[letter]

"*June* 15, 1915.

"There are pleasing, though very vague, rumours that leave has been reopened. We have promptly put in applications, but are not banking very heavily on it as yet.

"Things have been comparatively quiet of late, which is just as well. We have utilised the time to put out several more listening galleries, and I think we have these defensive galleries so well placed that they will not be able to get by unnoticed anywhere. Incidentally this gave rise to a good deal of excitement all on our own the other day. We heard working distinctly, and quite thought the Germans were nearly breaking in on us. Great panic! Immediate preparations for counter-charge—no time to be lost, &c. Then we woke up to the fact that it was one of our own con-nections a few feet away. Much relief and laugh-ter. But it just shows how jumpy we all are. It also showed how the imagination works. Several men were absolutely certain they heard German being spoken and boxes of powder being charged."

SUSPENSE

June 16.—Germans advancing very close to boreholes between 1A and 1D cross-cuts. Charged up with 140 lbs. and tamped 1A X-C. Listening in 1D. They were still working.

June 17.—1 A.M. Lieut. H. ordered to go and report on enemy mine fired in J3. Lieut. G. takes over at 3 A.M. Heard enemy working in A and D. Thought Germans heard to right of 1C.

June 18.—Germans heard in A, not heard in C.

[LETTER]

"*June* 18, 1915.

" M. went off with a very slight wound, but afterwards went sick, and was eventually invalided home to England for a time. He should be returning later on, and when he does I think there is some chance of leave. At least, our C.O. has promised to get it for us (H. and self) if at all possible. I think he recognises we have both been working pretty strenuously.

" This is particularly the case just now, as H. has been called off to help at another place for a few days, where the Germans have just been successful with a mine, I am sorry to say. Consequently I am without help here, and as it requires close attention I am putting in several days in the trenches until H. comes back.

" Leave, if we get it, will probably be five days, which means three clear days at home—not very long, but quite acceptable.

" I will, of course. let you know as soon as anything definite comes of it, but I shall probably not get much notice.

" I use the motor-bike occasionally to run into headquarters to discuss progress, but not very often. It is too bumpy on these roads for anything except duty trips.

" We are always on the alert for hostile mining, but, as you know, we have been able to detect all attempts so far."

June 19.—No more noises heard until late in evening. Lieut. G. then fairly certain heard them in C. Put in X-C to W of C and borehole. Lieut. H. took over.

(*Note :* The Mole was the only one who heard this particular sound, to the right of the C gallery for some considerable time, hence everyone else rather dubious about it. The men were always hearing noises, so their report did not carry any weight.)

June 20.—Nothing heard. Put in three more boreholes in A and D.

MUNITIONS

About this time the Mole received a letter from his business colleague, M.S.S., engaged on important munitions work, urging that the Mole could be of even greater service at home in view of his technical knowledge, and that he should make an application to be seconded for such purpose.

[LETTER]

"*June* 20, 1915.

" Herewith my reply to S., which please pass on to him after perusal.

" I should have no objection if the authorities can be convinced and if they order me home, but I must say that I do not think it probable.

" H. relieved me last night."

Letter (*referred to above*) to M. S. S.

" I have read your letter of June 16th with great interest. I quite see the force of your argument

and think your conclusion as to my greater useful-
ness at home may be correct, though possibly you
over-estimate my value in that direction.

" Whatever my own feelings on the subject
might be, it is quite out of the question for me to
take any steps at this end. To use a much-quoted
phrase : ' If they want me, they must come and
get me.'

" For good or ill I have taken on military
obligations, and can only obey orders. If I were
ordered to return home for service (industrial or
otherwise) I should not oppose it.

" If you can convince the authorities that it *is*
better to order me home I have no objection to
make."

On receipt of this M.S.S. put the whole
question before the Explosives Committee of the
Ministry of Munitions.

Holding Our Fire

June 21.—Nothing heard. Lieut. G. took over
at 10 P.M.

June 22.—Noise heard in C to west and face.

June 23.—Nothing heard. Lieut. H. took
over.

June 24.—Nothing new.

[LETTER]

June 24, 1915.

" Things seem quieter up at the mine. Appar-

ently they are sitting tight just outside our network
of defensive galleries. I am not surprised they
do not want to come any farther.

"Johnson, I believe, was killed by a stray
bullet in a communication trench—awfully hard
luck. I am glad Teddy G. is expecting to get his
commission. I can see now that it was quite a
mistake to recruit all these high-class battalions—
so many officers are required."

June 25.—Lieut. G. took over.

We Are Puzzled

June 26.—Brigade Mining Section attached.
(*Note:* For instruction.) Lieuts. W. and G—y
with fifty men. Lieut. G. reported noises opposite
X-C in C. (*Note:* To right), and also diagonally
from ahead to east. (*Note:* This last was something quite new and very disconcerting, as it
seemed to show an extensive system of defensive
mining in protection of the objective. This sound
was not confirmed until July 5th, and all rather
doubtful about it as far as anything to the left of
C was concerned until then.) Stopped face of C,
and started to cut powder magazine.

June 27.—Started X-C to east in C. Noises
heard occasionally on front. Lieut. H. took over.

Our Fears Confirmed

June 28.—Noises, undoubtedly due to mining,
heard at end of West X-C. Started new E shaft.

[LETTER]

"*June* 28, 1915.

" I return cutting from ' Engineering and Mining Journal,' which is quite amusing in its way, particularly as, instead of receiving ' military instruction,' we have people attached to us for their instruction, and as nothing but the verdict of a professional mining engineer will still the clamours of a scared infantry battalion when they hear alleged ' sounds of hostile mining.'

" H. will probably get his leave first, but when we do not yet know. It might be much delayed or, on the other hand, almost at once.

" Yes, Johnson was a splendid chap and deserved his honours thoroughly.

" The Germans took to plumping in shells near our billets a short time ago, so we have now got some huts built farther out, and have just moved into them. They are quite comfortable, though not quite so well equipped as our former home."

June 29.—Loud noises heard in listening post south of right end Q1, but can be heard all over surface, so probably not mining. Lieut. G. took over.

No Man's Land

June 30.—CX-C left stopped. Lieuts. G. and W. spent several hours during the day (*Note:*

Crawled out through grass) in front of Q1 trying to locate noise, crawling out about seventy-five yards. Came to the conclusion it was due to surface work.

Lieut. B. came to relieve Lieut. H., going on leave.

July 1.—Lieut. B. took over.

[LETTER]

"*July* 2, 1915.

" Leave is still indefinite, but there is a probbability in favour of the date already mentioned— arrival evening of July 7th.

" We have now attached to us two infantry officers and some fifty men to learn something about the work from us, so that they could undertake defensive work for their brigade if necessary, and leave us to deal with offensive work. They are quite keen, and will soon pick up enough to deal with ordinary situations.

" I had rather an interesting time the other morning. Some noises, supposed to be hostile mining, had been heard, so together with one of these brigade officers I crawled out in front to investigate. This was in broad daylight, but we could wriggle along in the long grass without being seen. We got threequarters of the way over to the enemy's trench when we espied a dug-out, and finally decided to investigate it. So we stalked forward (really with much trepidation) quite in the approved melodramatic style—business of cocked revolver and hoarse whispering—but eventually found it unoccupied and apparently not used for a long time. We eventually decided the noises were surface noises of some sort."

We Take A Chance

July 2.—C, made chamber at face and started X-C left to parallel enemy trench.

Note: Owing to absence of confirmation it was not believed that the enemy had got to the *left* of C, and it was intended to run a parallel from which short branches could be run to get absolutely under the enemy trench. As for the enemy working to the right of C, we were satisfied to let them come on, supposedly more or less parallel to C, as long as they were not aware of our gallery, and we could continue pushing on. This involved some risk, but we took the chance of picking them up again from our powder magazine X-C before they got very far or before they blew a camouflet on us.

July 3.—Lieut. G. took over at 6 P.M.

(*Note :* Thanks to communication trenches, it was now possible to get up by daylight. The officer relieving would motor-bike as far as practicable, going at full speed where under observation (to K.S.H.), and leave bike under cover at entrance to C.T. (near Voormezeele), where the outgoing man would pick it up.)

On arrival found bottom set of E absolutely wrong. Subsequently changed. (*Note :* A wail of woe over misdeeds of brigade section doing the work, as they were now supposed to be fully instructed.)

July 4.—C-XC left, advancing with special caution.

(*Note :* The Mole, still suspicious of enemy working and at the cost of slower working, took special precautions for secrecy and emergency action.)

WE BREAK INTO ENEMY GALLERY

July 5.—C-XC left broke through to enemy working.

(*Note :* Preparations in the way of getting filled bags ready for tamping, in view of some such contingency, had been done as far as possible. On breaking through, took immediate action for laying charge, &c.)

TO " BLOW " OR BE " BLOWN "? A TWO HOURS' RACE

Charged and tamped. Owing to advanced preparations beforehand this only took two hours; but they seemed endless, as one did not know what counter-action the Boche was taking.

WE WIN

Fired charge at 3.20 P.M. Smoke seen coming up behind enemy line, indicating complete success of blow-through. (*Note :* This unfortunately also revealed the fact of British mining operations here to the enemy.)

Lieut. B. took over at 10.30 P.M. (The Mole probably blessed him for being so late.)

[LETTER]

" *July* 5, 1915.

'' I now hear my leave may be postponed possibly one or two days. I shall not be able to conveniently wire before my arrival at Folkestone, but hope to be home shortly. I am going to try to make a running start and squeeze an extra day out of it by biking to Boulogne instead of waiting for the official train.

'' I have just fired another mine. It was meant to be offensive, but they have rather blocked our game by putting out defensive work. Still, we can yet give them a good shake up. This was very successful, as evidenced by our smoke pouring along their gallery and up their shaft.''

Serious News

July 6.—Lieut. H. returned from leave.

Lieut. B heard enemy on right of B, close to junction of new back-heading. Put in X-C nine feet. Enemy heard below. Also heard them under box heading to left of B. Apparently have run under B.

(*Note :* This was all grave news. The galleries had not been pushed out quite as far as wanted, and the Boche might blow Q1 *at any moment.* It was eventually decided to take the serious risk and push all work at utmost speed for the next day or so, when it was hoped to be sufficiently close to the various objectives, rather than fire a camouflet as a defensive move. This last would have greatly damaged our offensive preparations, and was therefore to be avoided if possible. Hence the decision taken, though all recognised it meant hazardous work.)

[LETTER]

" July 7, 1915.

" I am sorry to say leave is again indefinitely postponed, though it has been promised me for as soon as possible. It seems that a new divisional order limits the number of R.E.'s (of all branches) away at one time. Very annoying, but can't be helped.

" *Punch* has two very amusing series appearing from time to time. One is ' On the Spy Trail ' (Jimmy and his bloodhound), the other ' The Watchdogs,' supposedly written by some officer at the front. The last is very true to life, and is evidently written by someone actually out here. Curiously enough, the last to appear deals with a case of cancelled leave and ends up :

' Gott strafe all the powers that be

From Sergeant Blank to G.O.C.' (General Officer Commanding).

Like the nervous clergyman at the bank cashier's window, I heartily endorse this cheque.

" As a matter of fact, I hear that trains and boats are switched about now, crossing at night and obviating delay at Boulogne, so that when my leave does come off I shall probably drop the motor-bike idea I had. H., who got his leave in just before the new order, motored down, saving considerable time under the conditions then existing. The boat now gets in either very late at night or early in the morning—I am not sure which. In any event I should do my best to wire from Folkestone.

" My last note told you of another counter-mine fired, and it seems as if a further one will soon be necessary at one of our other places. The Germans are very persistent and have somewhat spoilt our offensive move, but we can still give them a really good shake up.

" Re service at home, we shall see if Munitions Department do anything. I am very sceptical, for the present at least. Possibly when the brigade sections are more trained there will be less pressing need for us.

" M. is still on sick leave, having some operation on his nose. However, a third officer, B., has been attached to us. One of us is to be available to help out a neighbouring division when wanted, but in the ordinary course of events we hope this will not be frequent, in which case we shall, between the three of us, be able to get a little more rest.

" The weather has been very sultry of late, ending up with a gale and heavy storm to-day.

" Our last mining exploit was quite exciting. I had heard various sounds, which I attributed to mining, but we could never hear anything very definite, and others had rather scouted my opinion. We were running a cross-cut from our main tunnel, and we actually broke through to the Boche gallery. Whether they did not see, or what happened, I do not know, but we were certainly able to hear someone working not far away. Not knowing what might happen at any minute, I lost no time in getting a charge in and tamped, a matter of about two hours. In the ordinary way it takes far longer than this, but I had everything practically ready. When we fired my observers distinctly saw a column of smoke about twenty feet high shoot up behind the German lines, showing that we had a clean blow through to their gallery and up their shaft. It must have done even more damage than usual. We have, as in this case, unintentionally cut things pretty fine once or twice. When it comes off all right it makes the result very successful, but it was really too close for comfort."

Can We Complete In Time?

July 7.—Lieut. H. took over at noon. Started

new small-size heading from end of **B** to due left, towards Snipers' House.

July 8.—Nothing heard. (*Note :* The enemy might be charging and getting ready to " blow.")

OUR BIG BLOW

July 9.—Stopped all headings and charged :

    1,400 lb. ammonal in new **B-XC.**

    200 lb. in old box heading.

    200 lb. in heading right from **B.**

    1,500 lb. in C face.

    150 lb. in C-XC right.

(*Note :* Existing charges in **A** and **D** were also to be fired.)

July 10.—Lieuts. G. and B. came up at 2.30 A.M. Fired at 3.30 A.M. (*Note :* This was the prearranged time, at dawn, when the enemy would be having " Stand to," and it was hoped that his trenches would be well filled. The infantry, Emma Gee (machine-guns) and gunners were to open fire after the " blow " if any enemy visible. H. fired the charges in Q1, the Mole in R1. They were fired, as arranged, five charges successively. After the first two " blows " the enemy machine-guns got busy, but from the third on not a sound. Evidently they did not know what was coming next, and fled demoralised. Our men must have caught a number as they went. There was a rain of débris into our own trenches, and theirs were, of course, much worse. **From**

the force of the explosion from the smaller charges
in Q1 it appeared that they had exploded enemy
charges of considerable size, confirming what had
been guessed at.)

R1 main charges very successful. Very large
crater blown reaching parapet. (*Note :* Charge in
C-XC failed owing to wires being cut by previous
" blows.")

Q1 also successful.

Lieut. H. left after firing. Lieut. G. stopped
in.

Entered C heading in the evening. Undamaged
for 200 feet.

July 11.—Very heavy shelling of **Q** and **R** in
afternoon. (*Note:* Reprisal for the mining.)
Enemy using large sausage thrower. Entered **Q**
shaft. Slightly damaged. D collapsed. B about
twenty feet open. Lieut. B. took over.

[LETTER]

" *July* 12, 1915.

" Leave news has varied almost from hour to
hour, but although I sent off a hurried note this
morning, which will probably reach you about the
same time as this, I now hear definitely it is to
be as follows : Start from here afternoon-night of
14th; arrive Victoria about 5 A.M., 15th (so do not
meet); leave Victoria 7 P.M. on the 19th.

" We have just fired some very successful
mines. We had two main mines and four smaller

ones. The net result of it was to destroy an obnoxious ' snipers' house,' blow up a section of trench and swamp a lot more of it with earth, and utterly wreck a lot of German attempts at mining. Altogether we fired off about 4,000 lb. of explosive. The Germans were scared to death and ran as if the Devil was behind them, so that our machine-guns were able to get in a lot of useful work. We did not attempt to take the trench, though it could have been done without difficulty —the trouble would have been to hold it afterwards.

" The sight was magnificent. With our main charges the explosion was terrific. The earth heaved up like a big pimple, broke with a tremendous flame bursting through, and then the earth shot up in the air for 200 feet like an enormous fountain. In one instance one of our smaller charges exploded a counter-charge in a German gallery which we knew to be alongside of us. We knew we had to take prompt action, and were putting forth every effort to get our main charges completed and ready for firing. The débris was scattered over a tremendous area, and we had to crouch behind parapets to protect ourselves. As the craters were about 100 yards away, you may imagine what it was like in the German trenches. The earth rocked like a ship at sea, and it is reported that one man was actually seasick !

" The men in our trenches were in great glee,

all up on the firing-step of the parapet and blazing away at the panic-stricken enemy.

" All the authorities are highly delighted, and the Commander of the 2nd Army Corps sent H. and myself a special telegram of congratulations, so we may yet figure as ' mentioned in dispatches.' "

Wind Up

July 12.—Many S.O.S. signals from P.N.T. and 23 trenches last two days. Nothing definite.

Leave

July 13.—Lieut. G. going on leave.

Enemy Active

July 17.—Enemy blew a large crater under road to right front of new shaft at 2.30 A.M., forty yards short. Twelve casualties. Small amount of gas coming through into Q galleries. (*Note :* Lieut. B. in.) Lieut. H. took over at 7 P.M. (*Note :* This gave rise to much strafing by the infantry, who could not see why operations over forty yards away had not been detected.)

July 19.—Germans heard knocking in crater over C at night. Probably driving piles. (*Note :* Heard in our gallery.)

July 20.—Again heard, but some bombs from trench mortar stopped them.

[LETTER]

"*July* 20, 1915.

" The trip back was uneventful and quite comfortable. I found the pseudo-Rolls-Royce (lorry) waiting for me when I got to railhead, and came straight on here, where I had breakfast.

" They have had considerable excitement during my absence. The enemy blew a mine some distance short of one of our trenches, but the débris caused a number of casualties to the infantry in the trench, I am sorry to say. The German artillery has also been quite active."

July 21.—Lieut. G. took over at 6 P.M. Again heard in crater.

July 22.—Again heard in C. Some noise reported in B. (*Note:* Apparently unfounded.)

COUNTER-CHARGES

July 23.—Lieut. G. at noon heard enemy close to WX-C in C. Started charging face of X-C, with 550 lb. Probably enemy had picked up their heading from crater.

Lieut. H. relieved at 6 P.M. Placed another charge in main C heading. Tamped. Enemy heard working all night.

WE " BLOW " AND ENEMY RETALIATES

July 24.—Fired at 6 A.M. Dull sober explosion. Both charges in series. (*Note:* i.e. " blew " simultaneously.)   Much timber blown up and near edge of old crater raised.

Enemy replied with .500 whizbangs, rapid fire. Nothing heard in B.

(*Note :* It would have been advantageous if the infantry could have occupied this crater.   As it was, being close to the enemy line, it was occupied by the Germans, who found it a very useful starting point for further mining operations.   They were driving piles, &c., without any attempt at avoiding noise, and could be heard most distinctly. Later on, after the system of raiding developed, a party would no doubt have been detailed to rush the crater and destroy the enemy works.)

Munitions Again

While the Mole was on leave his colleague, M.S.S., again put in an urgent application to the Ministry of Munitions for the utilisation of his services at home.   Shortly after his return to the Front the Mole received the following from W.R.P. :

" The following telegram was sent last night, but only delivered here this morning :

" ' Direct Lieut. G. call personally A.A.G., R.E., War Office, to-morrow morning.'

" I went this morning to the War Office and saw a senior officer, who, I presume, was the A.A.G., and explained to him that your leave expired yesterday evening.   He told me that it was only yesterday the Explosives Committee had handed him the papers relating to yourself, and having learned from them that you were on leave, and believing it extended until to-night, he thought that it would be better to see you here personally. Under the circumstances, however, the papers will be sent out immediately to Sir John French, and you will no doubt hear from him.

" He asked me what I thought your feelings were on the subject, and I explained I knew you would not like to leave the service, and if you were asked you would no doubt reply that they had the correspondence before them, and if they considered your services here were more important than at the front, it was for them to give the decision.

" I brought up the point that I knew you did not want to relinquish your commission, and he told me that under ordinary circumstances you must be either one thing or the other, but an arrangement might be come to whereby you were lent by the War Office (without Army pay) for munitions purposes, but at the same time retain your rank in the Army.

" He was exceedingly kind, and from a casual remark he passed I ventured to ask if he knew you. He said no, but that he knew all about your work ; that you were a jolly good man, and he only wished there were more of your kind at the front. This, I hope, will not make you too proud ! "

[LETTER]

" *July* 24, 1915.

" Please thank P. for the trouble he has taken and for his letter. I still feel rather sceptical as to any action being taken, as I know how reluctant they are to withdraw anybody from service in the field.

" I was not very long in getting on the job again. The night of my arrival there was one of the frequent panics in one of the trenches, and I had to go up to pacify them. The next night was my turn for our own work. We are again in contact with the enemy, and are firing to-day. . . . Just heard that it went off successfully. The Boches were evidently extremely annoyed, for they sent over about 500 whizbangs !

" The 5th Division, who have just shifted, wrote as follows :

" ' The G.O.C. 5th Division wishes, on the departure of the division, to express his appreciation of the work carried on by the 171st and 172nd Tunnelling Companies R.E. on the 5th Division front during the last four months. The companies have been in almost continual contact with the enemy in underground galleries, and consequently small mines and counter-mines have of necessity been fired almost daily by us or by the enemy. Difficult and trying situations have thus repeatedly arisen, to meet which quick action and steady nerves have been required.

" ' It is due to the devotion to duty and courage of all ranks that these situations have been dealt with so successfully.'

" After all that we are thinking of recommending the rabbit for a D.C.M. He goes on the job again to-night."

Ten Mines In Ten Days

July 25.—Got into C main to 175 feet.

Germans blew a large crater to right of C main, breaching old crater, 10.30. No damage. (*Note :* This was first of several enemy " blows," apparently due to " wind up," as they were too far away to hear or to damage us.)

July 27.—Lieut. G. took over at 6 P.M.

Enemy heard working in crater.

A Near Thing

July 28.—Lieut. G. to P3 and P4. " Wind." (*Note :* To investigate reports. Returned to working places.)

Lieut H. to 27 and 28. Very unlikely.

Enemy fired a mine between Q shaft and Mound, about 90 feet off, at 8.30 P.M. Damage to trench negligible. Two men in D, which partially collapsed. A chance of getting them out.

(*Note :* The Mole was about to inspect work in Q to measure up, &c., but as it was just on time for changing shift, waited on top to allow men to get out. Hence only two men caught. The whole of the shaft covering came down.

A Difficult Decision

Great excitement in the trench, as an attack was feared. Everybody up on firing-step blazing away. The Mole collected his sappers and, hastily calling the roll, ascertained two missing. Cleared the entrance to shaft. It was then a question as to course of action. If the mine was really close the gas would be through and have killed the two men, and would be deadly until well ventilated. On other hand, just a chance of rescue. After prohibiting any of the men from entering the mine, dropped down the shaft and found gallery in bad state of collapse and dangerous, air bad, but no gas; managed to worm up to first man, and found him living. Stopped all other work, and put best sappers on to rescue work. Owing to state of gallery only one man could work at a time and in short shifts.

Rescued

July 29.—Got first man out at 3.30 A.M. (alive).

Enemy working heard in crater at **R** in spite of 6-inch shelling. (*Note :* We had informed the siege battery that this crater was a good target, and asked for their assistance. After much palaver they got permission.)

Lieut. H. took over at 6 P.M.

Got second man out at 8.30 P.M. (alive).

Put in 12 feet bore and 50 lb. to right of C1.

[LETTER]

"*July* 80, 1915.

" Since writing last there has again been mining activity in our sector.   I believe I told you of the one that went up without any damage at all to our line and which we attribute to a blue funk on their part.   Since then they have sprung another one, rather closer to our line this time.   It did not damage the trench at all, but the outer rim of the explosion just caught one of our galleries; quite accidental, I think, as they were so far away that they could not have heard us, even if we had been making a lot of noise.   The gallery was badly crushed in, many of the timbers being broken, but fortunately none of the fumes from the explosion penetrated in.   Two of our men were caught, but by strenuous work we were able to extricate them both alive in the next twenty-four hours.   They were badly bruised and, of course, much shaken, but no bones broken.

" I was going around to the various working places to measure up progress.   I had reached the shaft, near which the enemy blew their charge, and, looking down, saw that a man was working on the pump.   I thought to myself I would not stop him but would wait for a few minutes until he had finished pumping, and walked a few yards away to where some new work was being started.   I was just looking at what had been done when I felt the characteristic rock of a mine and looked over my shoulder just in time to see the cloud of smoke shoot up. I made a running dive for the shaft, and, as soon as possible, investigated the damage below, quite expecting to find everything absolutely gone, but found there was just a chance to get into the face to rescue the men I knew were there and then came up to get a working party on to it as soon as possible. From the enemy's standpoint the result must be regarded as an absolute fiasco. The explosion took place just at dusk, and the enemy immediately commenced a heavy bombardment with much rifle-fire. It looked quite like an attack, and I must say the men in the trenches were very good. The customary ' stand-to ' at dusk was on and every man in his place and ready for action. In a few seconds everybody was pumping away with rapid fire as hard as they could go. While there was, of course, tremendous excitement there was no panic and there was no attempt to run.''

Rapid Fire

July 30.—Fired borehole at 11.20 A.M. and twelve rounds rapid fire from trench mortar into crater.

Charge just cratered in old one.

Got into heading in one hour and started long hole to left.

Enemy fired large charge in R crater 3.30 A.M. No damage.

Called to P4B re enemy mining, electric boring, etc. Man who heard it says he even heard talking, and would have heard what they said if he knew German. One was an officer because he had a refined voice! (*Note:* All pure imagination or noise from our own trench. Nothing ever happened there.)

July 31.—Fired borehole with 100 lb. at 12.15 P.M. Blew well in left wall of old crater. Lieut. B. took over at 6 P.M.

[LETTER]

" *August* 1, 1915.

" Mining has been very active of late. Since my last letter we have sprung two mines and the Germans one, which, however, did no damage. We had been able to hear them working in the crater, and, as they persisted in it, we were able to let them have it twice in twenty-four hours.

" H. has got his second star and well deserves it. He was, of course, senior to me, and I suppose mine will come along some time in the future. M., who was formerly with us, has now turned up again. The programme will now be as follows. H., as O.C. detachment, will look after routine work and generally supervise mining in our section, but will not actually take a turn in the trenches, though no doubt frequently up there. The other three of us will take it in turns—one day in the trenches, one day rest and one day on tap to help and advise neighbouring divisions.

" I have just figured in a new position : prosecutor in court martial. As I knew nothing of my duties it was fortunate I did not have much to do.

" The weather is very changeable. After considerable rain and fairly chilly weather, we are now having a scorcher again. There is no news at this end of the ' munitions ' application."

WE SUFFER

August 1.—At 12.35 P.M. enemy exploded mine in crater opposite R. Two sappers in C caught by 12 ft. of gallery collapsing. Started cleaning out and got to first man, who was dead, when enemy was heard in direction of East X-C. Noises heard suggested tamping charge. Probably the cross-cut was exposed. (*Note:* By enemy crater; blocked from our side) and enemy had got in. Heavy shelling started, and men were withdrawn. Shortly after another charge was fired by enemy, at 4.30 P.M.

Enemy fired large number of 6-in. and 8-in. A.P. (*Note:* Armour-piercing or delay action shells), evidently searching for shaft, but only scored hit on our dug-out.

At 10.40 P.M. a mine was fired in front of T1. No damage.

Enemy Makes Big Effort To Destroy Our Work

August 2.—At 9 A.M. enemy again heavily shelled us with 8-in., mostly A.P. Hit shaft and men's dug-out. All destroyed. R trench practically destroyed. Started repairing, when enemy again blew in crater at 3.30 P.M. Work resumed. (*Note*: Comparatively few casualties, as all men withdrawn to support trenches during worst bombardment.)

Lieut. G. took over. Six-in. shell on dug-out at E. Five sapper casualties. Sausages also used.

[LETTER]

" *August* 2, 1915.

" We have had a particularly trying time the last few days. The Germans have been exceedingly active, and in the last twenty-four hours have sprung three mines and given us a terrific bombardment with heavy stuff.

" Of the mines, none, I am glad to say, reached our trenches, but one was sufficiently close to one of our galleries to bury and kill two of our men. The bombardment damaged one of our shafts sufficiently to make it highly uncomfortable for us; it will require a lot of work to put it in shape again.

" As you will in the meantime have seen in the papers, they gave our line a very nasty smack on the left at Hooge."

A BAD STRAFE

August 3.—R again heavily shelled. Brigade Mining Officer (*Note :* The Mole caught him as he fell), his batman and Lucas (the Mole's batman) all wounded.

About 11 A.M. enemy blew to right of Snipers' House ; crater distant 50-60 yards.

Lieut. B. to N2 to investigate report of German canister (charged with explosive) found in borehole in our heading. Pure " wind." " Wind " reports also in Q2, T2, 23A, 27PC, and again, later, in T2 and P4.

Trenches again shelled in evening.

August 4.—Started shaft in T. Enemy used big sausages heavily in Q. Blew in parapet, but no damage to shaft.

A LET-UP

August 5.—All quiet in trenches.

[LETTER]

" *August* 5, 1915.

" At the moment I have nothing to acknowledge. 'Munitions' have now apparently put something to G.H.Q., as our C.O. has received an inquiry as to whether I was willing to resume work in England. My reply was to the effect that I was willing to do so, but wished to retain my temporary commission without pay. I expect it will take a few weeks to get it all settled up, but there is every probability that it will go through all right eventually.

" I cannot honestly say that I am sorry at the prospect in view of the fact that the authorities evidently consider my services useful at home. The past week has been particularly trying, and after practically a year of active service I shall not feel dissatisfied to let someone else take my place out here—for a time, at least, as it is quite possible that I might be ordered to the front some time later on again.

" We have been experiencing an intermittent but heavy bombardment for a number of days now, and that, together with the number of mines the Germans have been springing, though practically all harmless, has put my nerves rather on edge. Up to a certain point one gets hardened to the ordinary wear and tear of trench life, but of late I have found it more trying than previously. Casualties, I am glad to say, have not been too heavy."

[LETTER]

" *August* 7, 1915.

" The heavy bombardment they have been giving us has ceased, and things are fairly normal at the present time, that is to say, only the usual amount of ' hate ' (rifle and shell-fire) going on. Let us hope it will remain so for some time.

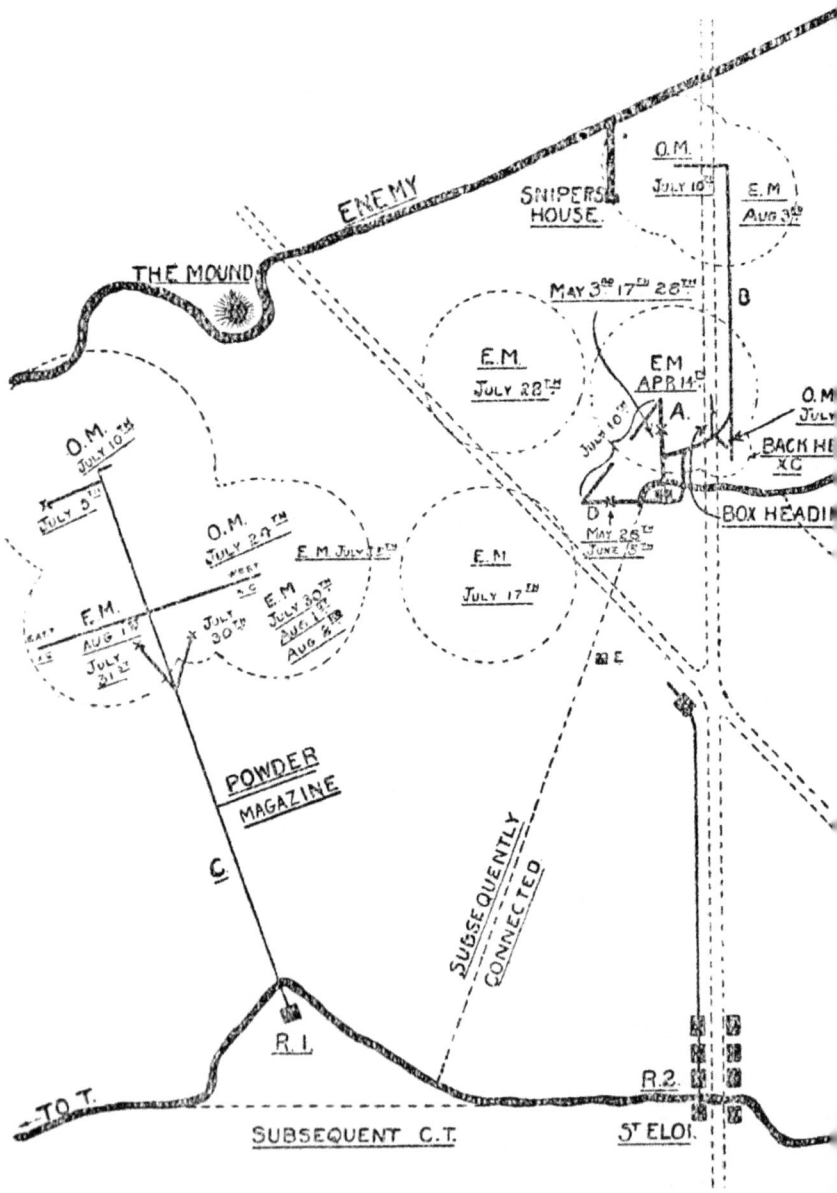

ENEMY

SNIPERS HOUSE

O.M. JULY 10TH

E.M AUG 3RD

THE MOUND

MAY 3RD 17TH 28TH

B

E.M. JULY 28TH

E.M APR 14TH

O.M JULY

JULY 10TH

A

O.M. JULY 10TH

BACK HE XC

JULY 5TH

O.M. JULY 20TH

E.M JULY 5TH

BOX HEADI

D

E.M JULY 30TH AUG 1ST

MAY 28TH JUNE 18TH

F.M. AUG 1ST JULY 31ST

JULY 30TH

E.M JULY 17TH

E.M

POWDER MAGAZINE

C

SUBSEQUENTLY CONNECTED

R.1.

R.2.

TO T.

SUBSEQUENT C.T.

ST ELOI

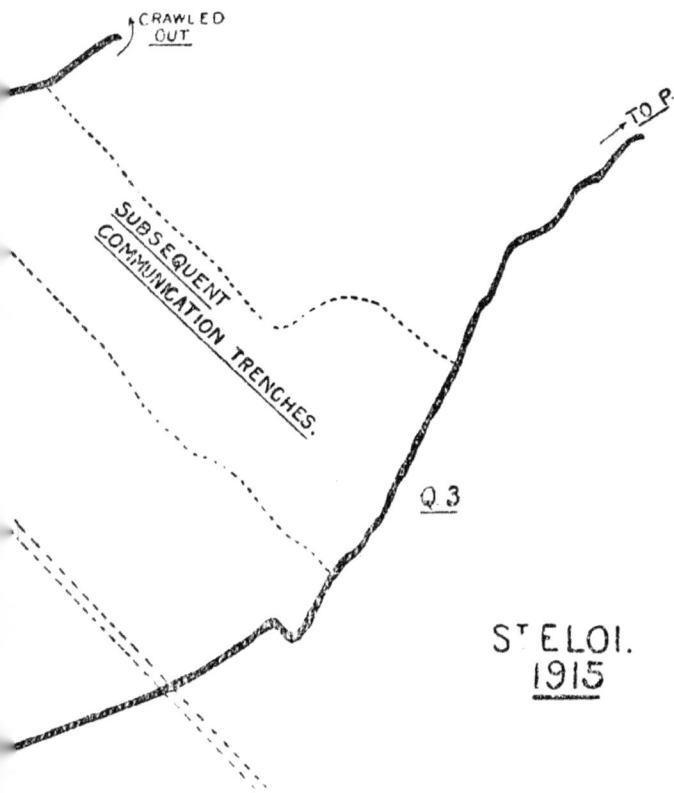

ABBREVIATIONS
X.— CAMOUFLET
M.— MINE
O.— OUR
E.— ENEMY.

SCALE
100 YDS

CRAWLED
OUT

→ TO P.

SUBSEQUENT
COMMUNICATION
TRENCHES.

Q.3

ST ELOI.
1915

" B., our third man, is going off with a crocked knee and is to be replaced by a substitute."

REPAIRS

August 7.—Noises reported in B, but nothing later.

August 9.—Attack at Hooge. (*Note :* By us.) Heavy bombardment from 2.45 A.M. At St. Eloi fairly quiet. We preceded bombardment by rapid rifle-fire which rippled all down the line from Kemmel to Hooge. (*Note :* During this period we were repairing damage done to R shaft by bombardment on the 2nd.)

[LETTER]

" *August* 10, 1915.

" I am now under orders to return to England and to report to the War Office. I am only awaiting a 'movement order' and railway warrant, which should be at hand shortly."

August 13.—Got into C.

August 16.—Enemy reported in C. Instructed to listen in magazine heading, and, if nothing heard, to push out south-west from end.

Enemy reported close.

August 17.—Nothing more heard in C until afternoon. Judged to right and down.

August 18.—Nothing more heard in C. (*Note :* Enemy blew crater opposite R on 24th.)

CHAPTER XV

MENTIONED IN DISPATCHES

SIR JOHN FRENCH writes in his dispatch of October 15, 1915 :—

" I desire to call attention to the splendid work carried out by the tunnelling companies. These companies, officered largely by mining engineers, and manned by professional miners, have devoted themselves wholeheartedly to the dangerous work of offensive and defensive mining, a task ever accompanied by great and unseen dangers.

" It is impossible within the limits of a dispatch to give any just idea of the work of these units, but it will be found, when their history comes to be written, that it will present a story of danger, of heroism and of difficulties surmounted worthy of the best traditions of the Royal Engineers, under whose general direction their work is carried out."

" *France,*

" *November* 30, 1915.

" To Field-Marshal Earl Kitchener of Khartoum, K.P., G.C.B., O.M., etc.

" My LORD,—In accordance with the last paragraph of my dispatch of October 15, 1915, I have the honour to bring to your notice the names of those whom I recommend for gallant and distinguished service in the field.

" I have the honour to be

" Your Lordship's most obedient servant,

" (Signed) J. D. P. FRENCH, Field-Marshal,

" Commander-in-Chief the British Forces in the field."

[EXTRACT]

MENTIONED IN DISPATCHES

ROYAL ENGINEERS

Tempy. Sec. Lieut. W. G.

The *London Gazette* Supplement, July 1, 1917.

CORPS OF ROYAL ENGINEERS

Temp. Sec. Lieuts. to be temp. lieuts. : W. G. Awarded 1914 Star, 1917.

Gower. CAPTAIN FLUELLEN, YOU MUST COME
PRESENTLY TO THE MINES ; THE DUKE OF GLOUCESTER
WOULD SPEAK WITH YOU.

Fluellen. TO THE MINES ! TELL YOU THE DUKE,
IT IS NOT SO GOOD TO COME TO THE MINES ; FOR,
LOOK YOU, THE MINES IS NOT ACCORDING TO THE
DISCIPLINES OF THE WAR ; THE CONCAVITIES OF IT IS
NOT SUFFICIENT ; FOR, LOOK YOU, TH'ADVERSARY,
YOU MAY DISCUSS UNTO THE DUKE, LOOK YOU, IS DIGT
HIMSELF FOUR YARD UNDER THE COUNTERMINES : BY
CHESHU, I THINK A' WILL PLOW UP ALL, IF THERE IS
NOT BETTER DIRECTIONS.

—Henry the Fifth, act iii., sc. 2.

GREAT WAR MEMOIRS, BIOGRAPHIES

Not for nothing has the First World War gone down in history as the most literate, and literary, ever fought. The products of mass education went into action en masse for the first time, and in the case of junior officers, the products of classical education went too. The result was an unprecedented mass of written material from the trenches. This a selection from our published stock that cover both sides of the wire.

MEDAL WITHOUT BAR
An English War Novel
Richard Blaker
9781783314249

1916-1918 A WAR DIARY
By H M Adams MC Worcester Regt.
9781783317271

THE ADVANCE FROM MONS 1914
By Walter Bloem with a Foreword by Sir James E. Edmonds
9781783317523

MY .75
REMINISCENCES OF A GUNNER OF A 75M/M BATTERY
By Paul Lintier
9781783317936

IRON TIMES WITH THE GUARDS
By an "O. E." (Pseudonym of Lt. G. P. A. Fildes, Coldstream Guards)
9781783312924

MERRY HELL! A DANE WITH THE CANADIANS
By Thomas Dinesen, VC
9781845740962

GUN FODDER
A DIARY OF FOUR YEARS OF WAR
by A.Hamilton Gibbs
9781845741686

OLD SOLDIERS NEVER DIE
By Frank Richards, DCM, MM.
9781843420262

LANGEMARCK AND CAMBRAI
By Capt Geoffrey Dugdale
9781845742683

MY WAR MEMORIES 1914-1918
By General Ludendorff
9781845743031

A BRIGADIER IN FRANCE
By Hanway R.Cumming
9781843421320

OVER THE TOP. A "P.B.I." in the H.A.C
By Arthur Lambert
9781843421269

AT G.H.Q.
By Brigadier General John Charteris CMG DSO
9781474538039